The Perfect Season

Roger Schafer

Dedication

This Book is Dedicated to My Father *"Roger Schafer,"* my Mother *"Barbara Schafer,"* and my two younger brothers, Michael, and Danny Schafer. They are and always have been Huge Baseball Fans. Mom and Dad spent countless hours with us while we three were younger, ensuring we had structure and sports as a huge part of our lives while growing up.

Acknowledgment

I am using this opportunity to express my gratitude to everyone who supported me in writing this book. Moreover, I would like to acknowledge you, the reader. Thank you for investing your time and money into this book.

About The Author

Roger *"Derby"* Schafer was born in New Mexico and has lived in Las Vegas, Nevada, most of his adult life. In the past, he played and coached numerous sports. As a Coach in Roller Hockey, his Team Won Nationals once and often had top teams competing on National Level for many years. He is the oldest of the three children in his family, all who reside in Las Vegas, Nevada.

Preface
The History Of Baseball

Baseball is a game played by a bat-and-ball between two opposing teams who take turns for fielding and batting. The game moves forward when one player, called the pitcher tosses a ball that a player from the batting team tries to hit with a bat. The primary objectives of the opposing batting team are to hit the ball into the playing field and to run across the bases. This is done by having its running players run to advance in a counter-clockwise pattern around the four bases to score. This is called *"runs,"* and you get points on the <u>runs</u> that you take.

The objective of the defending fielding team is to stop the opposing team's players from scoring the runs, and also to stop the runners' advance around the bases during the game. A run is scored when a runner legally proceeds around the bases in order and manages to touch the *"home plate."* The home plate is where the player began as a batter. The team that scores the most runs by the end of the game is the winner.

The evolution of Baseball began from older games that were played with a bat and a ball. These games were already being played in England by the mid of the 18th century. Baseball was brought to North America by immigrants, and that is where the modern version developed; it's the one that is played today. Baseball was widely recognized as the national sport of the United States during the late 19th century. It is a very popular sport in North America and has enjoyed a rapidly growing popularity in parts of Central and South America as well as the Caribbean. The game has become massive in East Asia, particularly in Japan and South Korea.

The evolution of baseball from older bat-and-ball games is tricky to detect accurately and will be a little difficult to track down from where it actually began. A general agreement once stated that the baseball played today is a development that took place in North America from the game played previously, known as the *"rounders."* It was popular in Great Britain and Ireland. In the book 'Basebal HYPERLINK "https://en.wikipedia.org/wiki/Baseball_Before_We_Knew_It%22Before"1 before we knew it.' A Search for the Roots of the Game that was written by American baseball historian David Block in the year 2005 suggests that the game originated in England. Recently discovered historical facts and figures support this position. Block argues that *"Rounders,"* and all the early versions of baseball were actually alternatives to each other based in different regions. He believed that the game's most direct predecessors are the English, mainly the games stoolball and *"tut-ball."*

The earliest known reference to baseball is in a British publication, A Little Pretty Pocket-Book by John Newbery, and it was written in 1744. Block discovered that the first recorded game of *"Bass-Ball,"* as it was spelled originally, was played in 1749 in Surrey. The game featured the Prince of Wales as a player. This early form of the game was brought to Canada by immigrants of English origins apparently.

There were reports of a variety of bat-and-ball games that were not able to be coded. These games were recognizable as early types of baseball played around North America by the early 1830s. Alexander Cartwright was a member of New York City's Knickerbocker Club. In 1845, he led the codification of the Knickerbocker Rules. While there are reports that the New York

Knickerbockers played games in the year 1845, the contest recognized it as the first officially recorded baseball game in U.S. history for a very long time. The game took place on June 19, 1846, in Hoboken, New Jersey. The *"New York Nine"* defeated the Knickerbockers with a score of 23–1 four innings in a row. The rules and principles of modern baseball continued to change over the next half-century with the Knickerbocker code as its basis. Professional baseball in the early 20th century had lower scores, and the pitchers were more dominant as compared to the present times. The dead-ball era, as it was called during those days, came to an end in the early 1920s with many changes in the rules and circumstances that were beneficial to hitters.

Strict new policies governed the size of the ball, its shape, and its composition. There was a new rule that banned the spitball and other such pitches that were dependent on the ball after it was treated or roughed-up with foreign substances. This resulted in a ball that traveled farther when it was hit. The rise of the legendary player, Babe Ruth, helped in altering the nature of the game permanently. He was the first legendary power hitter of the new era. In the late 1920s and early 1930s, St. Louis

Cardinals' general manager <u>Branch Rickey</u> decided to invest in many minor league clubs and developed the first modern-day farm system. A new league, which was called the Negro National League, was organized four years later in the year 1933. It was joined by the Negro American League. The very first elections to the National Baseball Hall of Fame took place in the year 1936. In 1939, Little League Baseball was founded in Pennsylvania. Now, baseball is widely regarded and recognized as America's favorite pastime sport.

Baseball has established itself in several other countries as well. The International Association featured teams from both Canada and the US as a professional league in 1877. While baseball is a sport that is widely played and enjoyed in Canada, many minor league teams are based in the country. The American major leagues did not include a Canadian club until 1969 when the Montreal Expos became a part of the National League as an expansion team. The expansion Toronto Blue Jays joined the American League in 1977.

Many European countries have professional leagues, as well. Out of all those, the most successful is the <u>Italian league</u>, founded in the year 1948. The Dutch league is highly renowned too. In 2004, Australia won a surprise silver medal at the Olympic Games. The European Baseball Confederation or better known *as "Confédération Européene de Baseball,"* was founded in 1953. It organizes several competitions between the clubs from different countries. Other competitions between national teams, were administered by the International Baseball HYPERLINK "https://en.wikipedia.org/wiki/International_Baseball_Fede ration" HYPERLINK "https://en.wikipedia.org/wiki/International_Baseball_Fede ration"Federation(IBAF). These included the Baseball World Cup and the Olympic baseball tournament.

This began in the year 1938 until its 2013 merger with the International Softball Federation to create the current joint governing body for both sports as well as the World Baseball and Softball Confederation (WBSC).

In the case of women's baseball, it is played on an organized amateur basis in several countries. After World War II, professional leagues were founded in many countries in Latin America. The most prominent of them being Venezuela in 1946 and the Dominican Republic in 1955. The annual Caribbean Series has matched the championship clubs from the four leading Latin American winter leagues since the early 1970s. These clubs include the Mexican Pacific League, Dominican Professional Baseball League, Puerto Rican Professional Baseball League, and lastly, the Venezuelan Professional Baseball League. In Asia, South Korea has a league that was formed in 1982, Taiwan in the year 1990, and China in the year 2003. All of these countries have professional baseball leagues. Baseball became a part of the Olympics as a medal sport in 1992. However, it was dropped from the 2012 Summer Olympic Games at the International Olympic Committee <u>meeting</u> that took place in 2005 even though it remained part of the 2008 Games. The serious lack of following of the sport in much of the world was a prominent reason behind Major League Baseball's reluctance to have a break during the Games.

MLB began the World Baseball Classic. It was scheduled to antecede the major league season, as a part of the replacement for the international tournament of a high-profile nature. The inaugural classic was the first tournament involving national teams to feature a significant number of MLB participants that took place on March 2006. The Baseball World Cup was discontinued after its 2011 edition because it was in favor of an expanded World Baseball Classic.

Baseball has been in the USA for the longest time; it came sometime around 1791. The game has nine players that begin on each team in the National League. The number goes as high as ten players in the American League with an assigned hitter. It was reported that Baseball began even earlier than 1791 in the town of Pittsfield, Massachusetts. The game was discovered because of an ordinance. It was created to ban playing baseball at a distance of 80 yards from the Town's Meeting House in Pittsfield.

In 1832, Baseball was seen to be played regularly on Saturdays in an area of the town that later came to be known as Greenwich Village. By 1857, sixteen New York areas devised an association and named it NABBP that stood for 'National Association of Baseball Players.' The union also included what has been known as the very first organization to govern the sport of Baseball. It also established a Championship that later came to be known as the World Series, both through the nation and worldwide.

The American League was created because of the growth and popularity of baseball in the country in 1901. We currently have around thirty professional teams in the USA, representing fifteen teams in the American League. There are close to fifteen teams in the National League.

There is a different format for both the primary leagues currently, i.e., American and National League. Each one of them has three divisions, with five teams in each division. These divisions are named *"East, Central, and West Divisions."*

In the American League's East division is the New York Yankee's, Boston Red Sox, Baltimore Orioles, Toronto Blue Jays, and Tampa Bay Rays. The Central Division of American League consists of the Cleveland Indians, Chicago White Sox, Detroit Tigers, Minnesota Twins, and Kansas City Royals. The American League from the West divisions each consists of the Oakland Athletics, Los Angeles Angels, Houston Astros, Texas Rangers, and Seattle Mariners.

The East Division of the National League East has the Philadelphia Phillies, New York Mets, Atlanta Braves, Miami Marlins, and Washington Nationals. The Central division of the National League has the Chicago Cubs, St. Lois Cardinals, Cincinnati Reds, Pittsburgh Pirates, and Milwaukee Brewers, whereas the Los Angeles Dodgers, San Francisco Giants, San Diego Padres, Colorado Rockies, and Arizona Diamondbacks belong to the National League West division.

Soon, each of these divisions will add one more team to it since it will happen to Major League Baseball at the beginning of the next season. It has been a long time for any expansion for all the teams, after all. Major League Baseball came upon the decision that it will be wise to keep it fair to have six expansion teams at one time. This is all by keeping in mind the growing popularity of baseball and the overall growth, the audience, and the increasing passion itself showed by the fans and admirers.

Every Major League Baseball Team has a combined total of 162 regular games every season each year. This principle was applicable to all the teams. However, it doesn't include the thirty-three pre-season games, and for two of the teams that make it to the playoffs, there will be at least another twelve games in case a team were to have a perfect playoff run.

There are more than 207 games possible for at least two of the teams. Of those teams, one would be a winner from the American League Division, while the other would be from the National League Winner. This was a feat that has still not been achieved before in modern-day history in any of the major sports. Another Feat that has never actually been achieved would be a team that has a perfect season during the regular season. That, in itself, has never occurred as of now. Yet, of all the things that have to happen in no way mean that they are unattainable. It's just that they haven't happened yet, but they will be and very soon hopefully. In the world that we live in today, baseball is played by hundreds of nations all over the world by both the genders. Many of these nations have their own professional leagues as well. Millions of young people all over the world aspire to play in major league baseball. They want to be a professional baseball player.

It so happens that, on a beautiful day, when the sun shines bright behind the clouds anywhere in the world, children and adults have a good time playing a game of baseball, and that includes women too. Then there are some parts of the world that are still blithely unaware of baseball.

The story takes place in the near future when it is announced that Professional Baseball in the USA would be adding six more expansion teams to create a total of thirty-six teams. Each division adds one team to each division, so every division has a total of six teams to begin the next upcoming season. Three of the six teams were to become part of the American League while the rest of the three play in the National League.

Contents

Page Left Blank Intentionally

Chapter 1
The Expansion

The baseball fever was now starting to gain immense popularity, and almost every city had started taking measures to make it to the upcoming season. Only six teams were to make it in the league, and all of them were to be one of the new three teams in the American League. Each team in the league was to have a twenty-five active player squad. Yet, all teams were permitted to have a forty player roster.

Each team was scheduled to play a hundred and sixty-two games. As six new teams were given a chance, the number of twelve hundred players was to increase to fourteen hundred and twenty players overall. That's more professional baseball athletes and more games. The number of games to be played then was five thousand, eight hundred and thirty-two in a regular season. This made the entire league more exciting and competent.

An increase in the number of teams had also increased the number of opportunities. Now, the new teams would not only need new talented players, but we're talking about an entirely new management team. From different types of coaches to medical staff and legal advisors, there were quite a number of openings expected. These expectations were not just to open up pathways for people who were to be associated with these fresh teams, but they were scope for other officials who could also be foreseen to multiply. Scorekeepers, security, and all other affiliates involved in the process were to be improved in numbers.

Teams employ hundreds of people to fill in for such positions almost every season. The jobs have different shifts and magnitude. For us to enjoy these games, there is a considerate number of people who are required to manage proceedings. While the six expansion teams might have a similar numbered team assigned for management concerns, the scouts are expected to be more, if not doubled, when compared to the ones who are playing. They would have less time in contrast to the job at hand in an extremely competitive environment.

The expansion teams were, by no means, favorites to even have a winning season, of all the different sports magazines and books. The *"Vegas Sports Book"* predicted no expansion team to win the World Series within a year of its formation, or even have a competitive team. Well sports bets have always been popular, haven't they?

Finally, the teams who were fighting for the spot had to be finalized. As planned, three teams each for American and National leagues were chosen, which were further divided in the East, West, and Central positions. The Cheetah's of North Carolina, Louisiana Nobles of New Orleans, and Albuquerque Conquistadors from New Mexico made it through to the National League in the East, Central, and West, respectively.

In the American League, there were the Invaders of Indiana, Oklahoma Owls, and Las Vegas Vipers in the East, Central, and West, respectively. These cities would have one of the six expansion teams, and by no means did anyone, fan or those directly involved, thought that any of these six new expansion teams would have a winning season or even make it to the playoffs.

To Win the World Series in 1st year would be an impossible task for The Cheetahs, Nobles, Conquistadors, Invaders, Owls, or the Vipers. They were all long shots with the odds of winning the World Series at 10,000 to 1 at a minimum, and as high as 15,000 to 1 in some of the

Sports Books. The new entries would have to make it through a long journey. Since they were new entities to the sport, their team-building task would be very critical.

By fabricating combinations and strategies from scratch, these teams were predicted by sports fanatics to perform extremely weak and have no chance for even a winning season. No one in the league was associated with Major League Baseball, and even the fans believed that not one of these six teams would even have a winning season or win half of their games.

If any of the new team wins, it would be very motivating for the other five because it has never been seen that a team made it in the league within one year of its existence. Before the idea of these expansion teams, it was not even considered possible for any team to make it in the playoffs in a league of this caliber. The best that may happen is within five years was that one or two of these new teams would be competitive, and it was maybe a possibility.

All the new teams had appointed over fifty or more scouts to seek out talent. Their talent hunt was not limited to individuals who had an interest in the sport, but any athlete who had the fitness and relevant talent would make it on the scout's list. Albuquerque Conquistadors, like all the other teams, were appointing scouts to find potential athletes. One of the hirees was Roger Schafer. The owner, Sheldon Winn, and General Manager, Bill Bell, were very keen to have an impact on the league. The team had Sheldon's complete attention. Roger Schafer was not hired on his consent. However, his general manager, Bill, was somehow able to convince him. Although the teams were directly preparing to be in the major league, they were still to assemble and formulate teams for minor divisions. This meant having teams for both the major league as well as the minor ones.

One team for AAA, AA, and A division was to be formed. One of the main reasons for doing so was to fill out for the *"farm teams,"* which allowed the development of talent and fitness. When a player faces an injury prior to joining the major team, he has to work back into shape and is gauged from his performance in the AAA farm team.

It gives a clear picture to the coaches on how well the player has recovered, and whether or not he has regained form. The scouting process for the rest of the teams was experienced. The teams which had been part of the game for a longer time had searched for talent in various parts of the world, mainly in places where baseball was popular. Sheldon and Bill, unlike the mainstream approach, had different plans for Albuquerque Conquistadors. They had signed the once well-known reputable scout, Roger, for a reason.

Roger Schafer was considered to have a very observant eye as a scout. His identification of talent and polishing skills were, by far, quite unquestionable. He was old to the game, and in his prime time, he had the credit of bringing great talent to the game. Roger had disappeared from the baseball scene, and rumor had it that he had stepped off because his skills and insights were burned out. It had been nearly twenty years for Roger to have functioned as an essential scout of a top club. He seemed to be a forgotten prospect.

Albuquerque Conquistadors, on the other hand, was hired as many scouts as possible, and this favored Roger in securing the job. His job interview left a great impression on the owner, Sheldon. The main proposition which he came up with was to visit places in search of potential baseball players where nobody had looked for before them.

The places had no limitations of being native to the sport. The criteria had no regard for the popularity that baseball had in any particularity or even any awareness for that matter. He wanted to explore new dimensions. At first, Sheldon was not confident with this idea and thought that the old scout was very ambitious. However, Bill talked him through an agreement to giving Roger a chance. Bill supported his argument stating, *"this would not be a waste of resources. If nothing else, we could consider it a unique marketing proposition. We would get new fans for the new team."* Finally, Sheldon was convinced by Bill's take on the matter and decided to give Rogers a green signal. Sheldon knew that all parts of America were under the scouts' radar for quite some time. Any exceptional talent might already be picked out, and this added more weight in Roger's approach.

Thus, they decided to start their search from places like Indonesia and Europe, and then move on to the other remote parts of the world. These locations were ideal for marketing. The small villages and remote areas were in abundance here. People would get familiar with baseball by Conquistador's name, and along with the marketing process, if they could find potential prospects, it would be the icing on the cake.

The first place Roger was scheduled to visit was Indonesia. A densely populated locality had a population of over two hundred and fifty million people. It comprised about 14,572 named islands and over 18,000 islands in total, which seemed like a nice place to start off with. The first stop on the scouting Journey was Jakarta. The capital city being the second largest of Indonesia in terms of population was a smart pick from the marketing perspective.

Since Albuquerque Conquistadors was a new team, they had a small fan base. The role of fans is very critical for a club to become successful. The support that a team might need would require time, which is based on performance. However, since the Conquistadors were new, they had to come up with a different approach. Roger starting off from Jakarta and now had been to various towns and villages across Indonesia.

Roger was there to find talent, and the idea of finding talent in these places was his own that he himself had started to question. It had been several weeks, and his motivation was dying down. He started to believe that the entire idea was a waste but was determined to carry out proceedings as per their plan. Bill Bell, the General Manager of Conquistadors, was constantly in contact with Roger.

Bill used to review his reports daily, but there was nothing substantial yet. Every day had a disappointing story. In light of how things were going, Indonesia did not seem to be benefitting their cause to an acceptable degree. They decided to shift their campaign from Indonesia to other places in Asia like Japan, the Philippines, and Korea. Baseball was never popular in any part of Indonesia, so visiting other parts of it would supposedly be serving their cause.

The trip to Indonesia wasn't as fruitful, so they had decided to move out from there in search of better results. It was agreed upon by Sheldon Winn to shift the venue from Indonesia to other countries in the region. Roger Schafer was recommended to book a small chartered plane and leave on a priority basis. This meant, the sooner he left, the better it would be. On returning to Jakarta from the village of Rappang, Roger was able to get in touch with a local pilot.

The pilot, Mahadiyi Suparman, was the owner of a small single-engine airplane. The pilot was to fly Roger to the Philippines, where he was to resume his scouting for Conquistadors. However, the plane did not appear appealing since it was old. It was hard to tell if it was a decent option to rely on for the journey, but Roger had limited options. The paint of the plane had faded off, and nothing else seemed in an appealing condition.

"Are you sure this will make it to there?" Roger asked Mahadiyi in an alarming tone. *"I can take you to the moon. My baby is very reliable. Don't worry, it will be fun,"* Mahadiyi replied, smiling calmly. Roger convinced himself that despite having no confidence in the plane, he was ready to go. He gathered his belongings and boarded the chartered aircraft. It steadily took off, and Roger was gradually gaining composure. It had been in the air for over half an hour, and things were going in accordance with the plan. All of a sudden, all the calmness and peace were blown away by a strange noise coming from the engine. Smoke started to appear, and the journey was only getting worse. This scared Roger; he had no hopes of making it out alive. The pilot immediately handed him a parachute. *"Hurry up! Strap yourself; this is all we got. Listen to me*

very carefully. I want you to pull the cord after counting till five. You can do this. Jump, and five. Jump, and five. Jump, and five."

Mahadiyi explained while holding his hand and taking him towards the only exit. Roger, however, was in a state of shock and had no clue about what was happening. The words coming out of Mahadiyi's mouth were meaningless. His brain had shut down. He somehow put on the parachute with Mahadiyi's help, then held onto the bag which was given to him by the pilot. The bag had few of his belongings and a satellite phone. Roger was so traumatized that he did not utter a single word throughout. The pilot, Mahadiyi, then pointed towards an Island. *"I want you to get there. You have to jump out. Jump and count till five. You have to get there. You can. Are you listening to me? You can."* he screamed in between the sound of the air and noise of the engine, which only got louder. *"GO, GO NOW!"* The pilot shouted to Roger and opened the cockpit door. Roger then was made to jump. As instructed, he counted to five and pulled the ripcord. On his way down, he witnessed the plane go down in the opposite direction. The heartwarming gesture of the pilot was captivating; he could have kept the parachute for himself instead.

However, despite being in a life-threatening situation on his way down, he made his way through the wind, being nothing but grateful.

Roger landed on the seashore and assumed to be in a remote location. There was not even a single person he could see. It looked like a place where no one had ever lived. The nightmare just seemed to have been partially over. He waited, lying on the beach, digesting| all the drama he had just experienced.

He unstrapped the parachute and transferred his weight from the parachute to the ground, which was all covered with dunes of sand. Without a moment's delay, the parachute caught up with the breeze as soon as the weight was lifted and floated back and forth until it was forced out over the terrain to the other side of the island.

Roger was moving his eyes around to sync with the parachute until it could no longer be seen. He grabbed the bag he had clung onto before jumping. The bag had baseballs, gloves, a camera, and a few other items along with a satellite phone.

He started to search his bag looking for the phone but was disappointed as soon as he found it. The hard landing had damaged the phone. He was now in an even more hopeless situation. He had no clue about how he would be able to find help. The place was alien to him with nobody around.

After thinking over and over again, he figured out his best shot was to wait until people started looking out for the missing plane. That would only happen after they realize it hasn't landed as per its schedule. He started gathering rocks, driftwood, and whatever he could find to fabricate a giant S.O.S on the beach.

He hoped that any plane that flew by would spot the S.O.S, and someone would be sent for his rescue. It was getting dark, and after three hours of hard work, all he was able to form was the 'S.' He was exhausted. It had been hours since he had eaten anything, and now he was hungry and extremely tired. The sun was setting, and the sensations of helplessness were all over his mind. He started looking for a place where he could rest for the night, hoping it to be the only one he'd have to spend there. He had no knowledge about this place and its wildlife, and so he did not know what to be prepared for. He chose a spot surrounded by stones on all the four sides and decided to rest there till dawn. It was a very long day, and he fell asleep in no time. The night had passed.

Roger woke up to a loud noise emanating from the plants and bushes. The sound seemed to have been caused by the strong wind. He noticed a giant boulder that wasn't there when he slept and thought that he was still asleep. The parachute was tethered to the boulder and was creating noises with the wind. He easily distinguished the sound coming from the parachute to being different from the one he woke up to.

As Roger approached the boulder and noticed footprints in the sand. These footprints appeared to be human, yet they were, by far, the largest footprints that he had ever seen. He started moving closer to the boulder and was breathless when he noticed two giant footprints. The depth of these prints indicated that the heavy boulder weighing in tons was lifted and placed there. He further assumed if someone had lifted it up, then they would have tied the parachute too. He heard a similar noise again. The noise was certainly coming from the bushes. He saw a glimpse of something moving. Somewhat afraid and not knowing what it was, Roger yelled out, *"hello, helloooo? I know you're there. Show yourself!"*

In reply, he heard a giggle from the left of where he was standing. And again, a chuckling sound. However, this time, it was coming from the bushes on the right side. All of a sudden, two young men that were the tallest that Roger had ever seen in his entire life, came walking out from inside the bushes.

Roger was stunned; the men were over eight feet tall. They had huge feet and hands, yet very slim athletic builds. He couldn't even guess their shoe size. They were enormous! The long muscular arms and strong overall built was unreal. *"Hello, I'm..., I'm Roger."* Roger started the conversation with his prominently disbelieving expressions. *"Hello Roger, I am Eko, the firstborn, and this is Indra, my younger brother and the strong one."* One of them said. Witnessing two such young men was enthralling, and since they spoke English, communicating with them was even more comforting. He had never seen any living person this huge. And it wasn't just one person; there were two, and both were completely identical. Roger asked in disbelief, *"Did you both carry this boulder together?"* Eko replied, *"No, Roger, I did it by myself. We tied this thing of yours, so it doesn't blow away."* Indra intruded, *"Yes, Roger, we found your thing near our village, and then we found you. You were sleeping. So we tied this so that it doesn't blow away, and you can have it when you woke up."*

Soon, they offered Roger food and water and took him with them. Roger started thinking differently. He asked them where they lived and what their hobbies were? He had realized that he had discovered what he was looking for. Now, all he was waiting for was to somehow get in contact with Bill and Sheldon even though he had only known the two identical boys for fifteen minutes. He still was very hopeful about committing them to something big. Bigger than all of them could imagine, including Roger himself.

Chapter 2
Eko And Indra

As Eko and Indra were leading Roger to their Village, he learned that Eko and Indra had been on the Island since they were babies. They were found by the leader of the Village, Idah, on the beach from an apparent shipwreck. Idah said that they were washed on the shore as infants and that they only had bracelets with the Names of Eko Suparman and Indra Suparman.

Idah instantly took them into her Village and raised them as if they were her own two children. They learned Indonesian, Chinese, Spanish, English, Hindi, Arabic, Portuguese, Bengali, and Russian. Idah's father was a *"Polyglot,"* a person that is fluent in Many Languages, and Idah's father had taught his only child, Idah, this. She then taught all the other Villagers as well.

This is how Eko and Indra were able to speak English and communicate with Roger. As they reached the village, there were only huts, and they lacked any modern items such as electricity, phones, computers, running water.

Rather, it was a simple life where they appreciated everything every day.

The visitor was something that they rarely had; they typically traded with several other villagers on nearby islands every several weeks. However, this village didn't have any boats or way to communicate with the outside world, and Roger would be here until one of the traders showed up. That meant a few weeks would pass before the next trading.

As they all reached the Village, Idah and the other villagers all Greeted Roger. Eko and Indra told them how they found him and that Roger would be a guest with them until help arrived. The first thing they all did was to offer Roger food and water, which was a blessing because he had not had anything since earlier yesterday. They all gathered around, and since they all spoke English, they were able to communicate.

Roger told them of how he arrived at the Island by sheer accident, and if not for that event, he wouldn't even have had stopped or scouted. After all, Indonesia has over 18,000 islands. After telling the Villagers of his events that led to why he was on their Island, he was asked what he was doing. Idah asked, *"Roger, what do you do?"*

"I am a Baseball Scout, and my job is to find Talent. I think I found that talent," Roger replied while looking at both Eko and Indra. Eko got curious now and asked, *"What is Baseball, Roger?"* To this, Roger began to tell all the villagers about the history of baseball and the game itself. The villagers had never heard of baseball except for Idah. She knew because, in her younger days, she did travel the world with her father since he was one of the top polyglot and often was hired to be a translator in different parts of the World. However, all the others have never even heard of baseball. The twins were fascinated with this game and wanted to learn about it. Since Roger was stuck on the island and had no way to call the outside world, he was going to teach Eko and Indra all about it.

Roger reached into his bag and pulled out a few baseballs showing all the villagers what a baseball looked like, saying, *"This is baseball."* He then pulled out a baseball glove. It wasn't even big enough for either Eko or Indra because their hands were gigantic. The adult-sized baseball gloves fit in the palm of their hands like an adult person holding a dime. Roger decided that, rather than just telling them, he would also begin to show them a "Baseball." He then gave one of the balls to Eko and told him to throw it to him. He pointed to his glove and said, *"Eko, throw the ball right into my glove,"* pointing into the open glove's pocket in the webbing. Eko instantly then threw the ball exactly where Roger pointed, yet the sheer force and power of the first throw broke a few fingers in Rogers's gloved hand. The baseball traveled so fast that he didn't even see the baseball approach. The breaking of the fingers put Roger in immense pain, and he cried out. Eko felt very bad and said, *"I didn't even do it hard. I am sorry, Roger."* Roger instantly thought, *"IF he didn't even throw it that hard and with perfect accuracy, then WOW."*

That knowledge certainly helped to block the pain; Roger was now excited and also learned that perhaps the only way to teach Eko and Indra is to have them work together as both pitcher and catcher. After all, no other person could even catch a pitched baseball by either one. Since the baseball gloves were too small to use both Eko and Indra, they told Roger that they were fine and didn't even need to wear gloves.

Roger then began to teach them both how to pitch and catch. Yet, what was even more impressive was that each time as Eko and Indra took turns pitching and catching, they threw the ball exactly where Roger asked them to pitch it. Even though he and the other Villagers couldn't see the pitch being delivered because of the speed, Roger could tell by the position of the baseball that they were the perfect pitches. Eko and Indra did this for several hours and didn't appear to slow down till later that day. Yet, they shocked Roger by then pitching with their other arm. Roger was shocked for he has never seen any baseball player, or pitcher for that matter, be able to throw a baseball with either arm; that too with such sheer force and perfect accuracy. This was more than what Roger had hoped for when his journey began. He knew that he had found, without a doubt, not just perhaps the greatest two baseball players ever; rather, he had just discovered the two greatest athletes ever.

As the sun was beginning to set, Idah declared that it was time for everyone to go back to the Village to eat and tell stories at the campfire; it was something they did every night. Since this was the first night that Roger was spending with the villagers, he was the storyteller and told them about more stories of baseball, which they all loved, especially Eko and Indra. The twins then told Idah that they wanted to be baseball players too. The next day, everyone in the village was up before the Sun rose, and they ate breakfast. As Roger woke up, he saw that Eko and Indra were both eagerly waiting for him to learn more about baseball. Roger then asked the *twins, "How fast can you each run?"*

Indra replied, *"Roger, we are the two fastest in our village, yet we do not know how fast we can run."*

Eko then said, *"Would you like to race us, Roger?"*

"No, not I, I do not want to race against you two. However, how about you two race against each other?" Roger suggested. Both the boys started grinning and said, *"OK, where do you want us to race around the island?"* they asked.

"Sure, if you want to race around the island, then do that. Get Ready, Get Set, GO!" In less than a few seconds, they each ran around the entire island to a tie.

Roger only knew what he saw of the Island while he was flying in the plane. Before the crash, he didn't know exactly how big the island was that Eko and Indra had just raced around. So the three of them decided to walk the entire Island on the path that they had just raced. '*It must have been a total of 2-3 miles, '* Roger thought as they finished the walk around the path they raced earlier. Now Roger learned that they were also the two fastest humans ever.

As they went to a part of the island, Roger learned that, while he was sleeping, Eko and Indra had cleared out and made their own baseball field to learn more about the game. They had even created all the bases and home plate, a pitcher's mound. A highly impressed Roger checked and adjusted the bases and pitcher's mound to what was near the exact measurements that were used in baseball.

From Home to the 1st base was 90 feet, 1st base to 2nd base was 90 feet, 2nd base to 3rd base was 90 feet, and from 3rd base to home plate was another 90 feet. The pitcher's mound to the home plate was approximately 60 feet and 6 inches apart, which was the same distance in Major League baseball. As they finished the corrections and made minor adjustments, Roger was ready to begin *"Baseball Practice."* Roger first taught them the importance of stretching and warming up.

They then decided to try some base path running drills. This is where they were in the batter's box, which was completely covered due to the enormous size of their feet. Roger, Eko, and Indra stood in a batter's stance, and then because they didn't have any baseball bats, they pretended that they hit the baseball. When Roger said, *"GO,"* they would leave the batter's box and touch all the base's in order until they returned to the home plate. Eko and Indra did this on either side of the plate, as a left-handed hitter, or a right-handed hitter, every time under a second. They did this for a few hours, and neither Eko nor Indra slowed down one time. They moved so fast that it was nearly impossible to keep up with them by a naked human eye.

Eko and Indra then wanted to do some more pitching and catching with the little time they had before the sun was going to set. Idah, of course, wanted everyone back at the village by nightfall. It was just like the day before, but this time, it was with the pitchers' mound, and with a plate set up near the exact measurements, they began to take turns pitching and catching.

Roger was amazed by the perfection in the accuracy and decided that even with a broken hand, he would go to the batter's box and pretend that he was a hitter. He wondered if they could still pitch with perfection with a person in the batter's box? Concerned for his fingers on his catching hand were still broken from yesterday, Roger was, to say the least, nervous.

Yet, after a few pitches, he became far more comfortable and then switched to the other side of the plate to make sure that they could still pitch regardless of the position. Eko and Indra did not fail or have any problems pitching to either a right or left-handed hitter.

Then Indra said, *"Roger, do you want me to pitch you three in a row? To, as you said, Strike You Out?"* Roger replied, *"Of course. I will be ready when you are, Indra."*

Indra said, *"Ok! Get ready, get set, GO!"*

Eko quickly screamed, *"Roger, You're Out."*

A very confused Roger then said, *"What do you mean, Eko? That was only one pitch."*

Indra said, *"No, Roger. I just pitched you three pitches, not just one, and you said there are three strikes, then you're out."* Eko confirmed that Indra had just thrown three perfect pitches when Roger thought that only one pitched was made. Roger knew right then that these two, if they do play baseball, would indeed be the two best baseball players ever to play the game.

Who could even hit a pitch? They pitch too fast even to swing or see the baseball. Yet, what could they do as batters? On the journey from the practice field to the village, Roger told the twins, *"I wish we could have a baseball bat for that is the one thing we do not have, and I would love to see what you two could do as hitters."*

As they arrived in the village, right before the sun was setting, as expected by Idah, Roger described what a baseball bat looked like and how it was made from wood. After eating with all the villagers, they wanted to hear more stories from Roger. However, time was running late, and they all went to sleep. It was now the third day on the island, and as Roger woke up, he was shocked to see four handmade baseball bats that Eko and Indra had made while he was sleeping.

They weren't perfect, yet they were certainly better than nothing. Eko and Indra wanted to make sure that at today's baseball practice, they would be able to hit since that is the one thing they had yet to do. As they finished up with the warm-ups of stretching and playing catch, Eko and Indra were excited to try hitting finally. What was amazing was that the bats, even though they were close to the standard league size, the bats were like a grown man having a pen in his hand.

Eko and Indra, in the teaching of hitting, didn't even use both hands to hold the bat. Rather, when they were learning to bat left-handed, they only had the bat in the right hand. And while learning to bat right-handed, they only had the bat in the left hand. They simply flicked the baseball bat one-handed while learning about hitting without any actual pitches. Being exceptionally fast learners, they were now ready to hit, and Eko, being a senior and first, was to bat first with Indra catching and Roger pitching. Since Roger's catching hand had broken fingers, he asked that Indra roll the balls back if any pitches were not hit by Eko.

One, he threw the ball, Roger winded up and delivered the first-ever pitch to Eko, and with a swat of his arm (not even a full swing) BLAST! The ball was traveling so far and so fast that Roger didn't even see where it landed in the ocean. Instantly, Indra raced off in the same direction the baseball went, and in just a matter of seconds, Indra was back with a wet baseball after it landed in the Ocean. Roger was shaking his head in disbelief, yet he knew what he was seeing was true and real.

Eko continued to hit the ball and always got the same results. Then Eko decided to try to bat on the other side, just like pitching with either arm.

The results were the same, either as a left-handed or a right-handed hitter; each pitch was a blast out to an area so far to see with the naked eye. Now, it was Indra's turn, and just like his older brother, Indra too had the exact same results. Hit after hit, and Eko, like Indra, went out into the ocean to retrieve the baseball in a matter of moments. Within a week of their first meeting with Roger, Eko and Indra resembled some seasoned baseball veterans. The only difference was that they were eight feet and eight inches tall right at the age of nineteen and could run, throw, and hit faster or harder than any other human knew of all time.

Without any communication and knowledge, one of the villages were soon to arrive for trading goods, and Roger would soon be able to leave the island and get in touch with Sheldon Winn and Bill Bell at the Conquistadors once he reached the place with phones or internet. However, Roger was worried about two things; the first was that would Idah approve of this? After all, Eko and Indra had never left the island since they first arrived from some shipwreck as infants. The second concern was "*IF*" Eko and Indra were found out prior to the draft, then they could end up on a different team, or one is drafted to another team. For this to work, Eko and Indra need to be on the same baseball team. After all, no other person could even catch a pitch from either one without any serious injury, as Roger had learned from his personal experience. It was the last night on the island, the evening before the traders were to arrive early the next morning. Roger and Idah stayed up all that night to discuss the future and also talk about Idah's approval. For Idah was the only person in the tribe, besides Roger, to know what life outside the Island was like, and of course, she being their mother was naturally concerned.

They agreed that the next day, when the other villagers they trade with arrive, then only Roger would leave the island. This was to let Sheldon and Bill know that he was still alive since they had lost contact since the plane crashed. That call would also include news of Eko and Indra. Roger knew that both Eko and Indra would be playing baseball for the Albuquerque Conquistadors together on the same team at the start of the upcoming baseball season. Eko and Indra would obviously do exactly as Idah and Roger asked of them; after all, Roger had become somewhat of a father figure to Eko and Indra, just as Roger had grown very fond of Eko, Indra, and Idah.

But until the draft was over, and he made sure that both Eko and Indra were Conquistadors, they would stay with Idah and the other Villagers until in a week or two at the latest when Roger returns to the Island. As Roger went through his items, he made sure that the camera was with him, for that was his only proof of the Eko and Indra. The pictures and video were to show Sheldon and Bill about his discovery.

As the other village boat arrived, Idah was the first one to greet the Captain, and since Roger didn't speak any of the Indonesian languages, he confirmed with Idah that the Captain would indeed make a stop at a place with a phone or internet. They would be able to show exactly where on the map the Island was.

Idah indeed let Roger know that he would be going with the Captain and his crew to a place that, when they arrive, they would have a person that spoke English. He would have to make sure where our home was. As they all said their goodbyes, Eko and Indra began to have tears, for they would miss Roger, and so would Idah and the other villagers. Roger would miss them all too.

Chapter 3
The Village

The boat was slowly getting smaller for the villagers standing on the shore as it was moving away into deep water. Roger was waving his hand, and soon, the village disappeared. Roger was now in open water. The stay in the village was very unreal for him. He had survived the plane crash and then met two incredibly huge and strong young men who had unnatural features and strengths. It would have been difficult to believe for anybody.

There was nobody that he could talk to because nobody on the ship knew English. All he could do was sit and recall every moment that he spent on the village. Besides the village memories, the only other thing that he could think about was the fortune that Eko and Indra could bring to the club. He believed that there was a reason for all of it to have happened, and he was very impatient to break the news to Sheldon and Bill.

He was in the middle of the sea with a bunch of men that he couldn't communicate with, and the water all around was making the scenery a boring one. Captivated by his thoughts and vision, he soon fell asleep. It had been over two hours, which was half of the total journey time as committed by the Indonesian captain when a loud horn of the ship woke him up. He sat up straight and started looking to spot the ship where the noise came from.

One of the crewmembers noticed and pointed behind him. Roger turned around and saw a huge ship with the British flag. He was very happy to see the ship. It was obvious that someone on the ship would definitely know English. He somehow managed to converse with the captain, mainly through his actions and asked him to take him to the ship or gain its attention. The Captain went close to the ship that was noticed by the crewmembers. When the distance was close enough for Roger to be heard, he started in a loud voice.

"I'm Roger Schafer from America."

The captain responded by giving his details and then inquiring about the reason that Roger wanted to speak with them. Roger then briefly explained his story to what had happened and how he lost contact. The British captain, without any hesitation, welcomed him on board. Roger started thanking the Indonesian captain and his crew and then moved to the British ship. The British ship was full of refreshments and had the communication technology that Roger had desperately been waiting to get his hands on. He was served with refreshments right away. Roger was lucky right from the moment he had left the States. The group of people he had run into throughout the campaign were very cooperative and hospitable, and he found out that the ship was heading to a port in Singapore.

Roger then had enough time to tell the captain about his story. He was allowed to use the communication facilities onboard to make contact with Conquistadors. He attempted to reach their main office in Albuquerque, but due to the time difference, he wasn't able to get in touch with any of the officials. After making several tries, he was disappointed.

It was late at night in Albuquerque, and to expect someone to answer the office phone was not very sensible. He left a message on the answering machine hoping to be contacted immediately. The message contained the ship's information and the time of arrival. He was now only to wait for the ship to get to Singapore.

Roger was excited and worried at the same time. He was excited to tell Sheldon about the talent he had discovered. It had been a month since he had last spoken to either of the owner or manager of Conquistadors. It was in Indonesia where he had last been in touch, informing his authorities about the course of a campaign which was very disappointing. He wondered if he still had the job. Once they found out about his discovery, he was confident that he would be appreciated. The discovery was indeed amazing, and the Conquistadors were definitely not going to miss this opportunity.

It had slightly been over a month since he had last known what was happening around the world. He was at a village that did not have any means of communication. The people living there had no clue about what was happening in the world; neither were they concerned. He was very curious to get updated with what had happened in these past few days. As a baseball personnel, his interests were more concentrated on baseball news. The league was on the verge of its beginning as per schedule, and this is why he was very eager to get back. He wasn't really worried about the job anymore; he had realized that what he had to offer could earn him enough to sit and relax for a lifetime.

He started thinking of ways that he could make the most of them. Before his scouting journey for the Albuquerque Conquistadors had begun, he wasn't very optimistic about their coming performances in the league. He felt the odds were against them, and it seemed very difficult to make it to the playoffs. However, things would change on his return. The ratio of the odds would drastically be reversed after he had discovered Eko and Indra. They were unique and powerful, and Roger was electrified to introduce them to the baseball world.

The ship was approaching the port, and Roger was very hopeful of finding someone from Conquistadors to be there for his reception. As he made his way out of the ship looking for someone from his baseball club, he spotted a young lady holding a board with his name written on it. He directly went to the young lady and formally introduced himself.

"Hello, I am Roger Schafer, and you are?"

"Hi, Roger. We are glad you're back. My name is Aspyn Walling, and Sheldon Winn has sent me. I was asked to

make sure you arrived safely, and I'm here to get you home. You do have your passport. Don't you, Roger?" Aspyn introduced herself and then elaborated on why she was there.

The owner of Albuquerque Conquistadors had nobody in his family except his niece, Bernice. They both were close, maybe because all they had was each other. Aspyn Walling was Bernice's best friend and assistant. The league's pre-season was soon about to start the final supplemental draft for the upcoming season, and all the New Expansion teams had tough schedules. This was the reason that Aspyn was sent to prepare for the upcoming Season.

Roger replied, *"Yes, I do, and I thank you for being here. Also, please let Sheldon and the organization know how much I appreciate this."* he continued with the story of what had happened in the past month, careful never to mention anything about Eko or Indra.

This was the first time that he was telling it to someone related to baseball, and this was just the beginning of the many more times that he would tell. He knew that he could not tell this to a lot of people and that if he did tell others about Eko and Indra, then they might find out themselves. This would ruin the plans to draft both Eko and Indra on the Conquistadors. Yet, when the time was right (after the draft), he would be ready to present the Indonesian sensations. Then everybody was going to believe.

"Come on, Roger, let's take you home," Aspyn replied, and both of them started walking away from the pier towards the waiting parked car. They left for the airport straight to where Sheldon's private jet was waiting for them at a private airstrip for Jets. He was finally going to fly back. The moment he stepped on the plane, he was struck with memories of Mahadiyi Suparman, the Indonesian pilot. It was not a journey that he would want to remember, and the decision of the pilot of considering the aircraft being fit to fly was indeed very vacuous.

But the way that Mahadayi then reacted to the situation and saved Roger's life and giving up his was a gesture that he was to remember for a lifetime. The plane that he was now traveling in was to take him to Albuquerque and was a thousand times better than Mahadayi's. He had traveled a long distance and was hoping for this to be the last phase of his journey. It was a fifteen-hour-long flight, and he prayed the entire journey to land safely.

After the long and tiring flight, he was finally at the Albuquerque airport. While he was relieved, there was anxiety piling up inside of him from when he first landed on the island in Indonesia. He had begun to think that he might never get home. He had to make his way through hunger and traveling in seas to being disconnected from the world. It had exhausted him both physically and mentally, and from the moment that he stepped out of the airport, he was relieved to have made it back. Sheldon's attorney, John Slyvestri, and Sheldon's closest friend, Barbara Sue, were waiting at the airport to receive them. Barbara was Sheldon's oldest friend and advisor. He would never make any decision without consulting her. They were childhood friends, but their friendship gained meaning when they had grown into adults.

She had been beside Sheldon from the beginning of his career. They headed for the stadium to see that the new stadium was nearly completed for the upcoming baseball season. Roger greatly admired the arrangements that Sheldon had made for his safe return. He wanted to thank

Sheldon, and more importantly, inform him about Eko and Indra in the near future.

There were less than twenty-one days left in the submission of the draft, so the stadium had to be completed before that. Sheldon, along with his manager, physician, and head doctor of the team, was at the stadium. They were busy in finalizing the team and analyzing the fitness of the players who were to be offered contracts. As soon as he saw Roger, Sheldon jumped up from his chair in a welcoming manner. Roger felt his job was safe and that he was still employed, but only if he still wanted to be. Sheldon said welcomingly, *"Roger, I'm so glad that you're back. The last I heard about you was that you took some flight for Singapore and then you disappeared. Honestly, we thought the accident had cost you your life! Anyhow, welcome back, Roger."*

Roger thanked him for all that he had done and started off with the story of the plane that never landed. He did not inform anybody about Eko and Indra and kept that as a secret. He had an excellent reason behind it. Roger wanted to be fired as a Scout and then be the agent for both Eko and Indra; Roger was to make smart to consider negotiations for himself. Everyone there heard his story, and they were all in disbelief to how he had survived.

"If it weren't for the pilot, I wouldn't have made it." Roger ended his story.

It all sounded unreal, like a scene of a Hollywood movie. Roger could tell this from their expressions, but he was more concerned about the reactions of Sheldon, Bill, and Barbara when they find out about the Idah's children. If they were having a difficult time visualizing the story of the crash, then it would be near to impossible for them to visualize Eko and Indra. They might even think that there was something wrong with him or that he had lost his mental stability, he wondered. He decided to put off telling them about Eko and Indra at that moment.

"Sheldon, you will have to fire me if you want your team to end up as champions." Roger continued.

Sheldon replied, *"I don't understand. Are you serious?"*

"Yes, if you don't, then I'll quit. You've been very nice to me, Sheldon. I want your team to win the World Series in the very first season."

Sheldon was getting confused, *"That's very nice of you. But how can I expect that to happen if you quit?"* he said with a smirk on his face.

"I have an amazing thing to offer, the greatest thing I have ever experienced or witnessed," Roger said with confidence.

"I don't know what you're up to, Roger. What do you want, and what do you have?" Sheldon had become curious.

In fact, the entire staff had. It seemed that either Roger had lost his mind or that he had found a Superstar who was to play for the Conquistadors.

"Five million dollars," Roger replied straight away without any hesitation.

They were all now in a state of shock. Their expressions were sufficient to understand their state of skepticism. Roger Schafer was an experienced scout who was once known as the best in the business. If he has not lost his marbles, then he definitely had something valuable under his sleeve.

Sheldon did not react. His expressions were stagnant, unlike the rest.

"I don't know, Roger. You expect me to pay you five million without even knowing what I'm paying you for?"

"Write me a check; I'll come back in three days at the same time and show you what I have. If you don't like it, then you can have every single dollar back. It won't cost you a penny, Sheldon if you don't like it, which you definitely will. But what it'll earn you is the World Series title in season one, and probably for many years after that."

"It better be worth five million," Sheldon replied.

He asked Barbara to prepare a check and ordered John to prepare the papers. In a short duration, both the things were taken care of, and Roger and Sheldon signed the contract. Roger had become unemployed by his own will, and the negotiation was the reason why. The check was presented to him by Barbara, and the meeting was scheduled for three days from that moment. They both shook hands, and Roger left.

Instantly, Roger went to the bank in Albuquerque, where Sheldon had an account. After verifying the check was legit, the bankers deposited the money into an account that Roger had just created. He then decided that he would go to

Las Vegas, Nevada, where the Sports Betting was legal. After arriving at the airport in Las Vegas, Roger took a cab to the MGM resort near the airport.

Roger went directly to the Sportsbook and asked if the manager would meet him, for he wanted to make a large bet on this upcoming season World Series champion. This is called a future bet as to who will win the World Series in baseball prior to the season starting. When the Sportsbook director arrived, he said, *"I understand you wish to place a bet on the Futures for the World Series. How much do you wish to bet, and on which team will you be betting on?"*

Roger replied, *"I wish to make a bet on the Albuquerque Conquistadors to win it all this season if I get the odds which currently stand at 16,000 to 1."* The Sportsbook director looked at Roger and said, *"OK, if I give you those odds, then how much do you wish to bet?"*

Roger replied, *"Three million dollars."*

The sports bet director then, based on how the Conquistadors were the longest odds-wise to win the World Series at that time, decided to take the bet. After all, with the regular draft held a while ago, the Conquistadors based on the current roster were the team expected and predicted to finish in the last place in the National League and also have the least amount of wins in the entire league.

Till then, no one knew of Eko or Indra yet, and this payout to the sportsbook director thought was an easy win for the MGM Sportsbook. The director decided to accept this bet, knowing that if the Conquistadors do win, Roger would have a winning bet to collect 48 billion dollars.

They made a bet, and instantly after that, the odds for the Conquistadors instantly dropped at all MGM Casinos and MGM Sportsbooks to 8-1 to win it all. Quite a few others had noticed this big change, and this caught the attention of many baseball fans and others in Major League Baseball, including Sheldon. Roger then left the MGM casino and headed back to the airport to leave back to Albuquerque.

He had a meeting that next day with Sheldon, Bill, and Barbara. As the meeting was getting ready, Sheldon was somewhat upset, for he knew that Roger took that money because he was the person to make this bet. Sheldon wondered if he just lost five million dollars, or at least three million since that was spent making a bet.

Roger arrived ten minutes prior to the agreed meeting time, yet Sheldon, Bill, and Barbara were already waiting for Rogers's arrival. Upon seeing him, Sheldon said, *"Well, Roger, I know that you made that bet on the Conquistadors to win the World Series. It was you, wasn't it?"*

Roger replied, *"Yes, Sheldon, that indeed was me who made that wager. And as you know, since you did fire me two days ago and the bet was made yesterday, while I was not an employee of the Conquistadors or any other baseball team, then it wasn't a violation."* After all, baseball had a strict policy against anyone involved, *"Players, Owners, Coaches on betting baseball...it is illegal and against the league policy."*

However, Roger made this bet 100% legally since he was not affiliated with any professional team at the time.

Roger said, *"Sheldon, don't worry about that money, let me ask you; how much would you pay to win the World Series this year in our first season ever?"*

Sheldon replied, *"One hundred million dollars to win it all in season one is what I would pay, Roger."*

Roger smilingly replied, *"Well, I just saved you 95 million dollars."* Roger then pulled out the camera, and then he started telling Sheldon, Bill, and Barbara about Eko and Indra what they did while he was on the Island, teaching them baseball and what they were capable of. Everyone was stunned, still glued to the pictures and video that Roger was showing them of Eko and Indra.

Bill was the first to speak, *"Well, the supplemental draft is about to happen, and since that is yet to occur, the best thing we need to do is keep both of these guys quiet until after we draft them next week."*

Roger replied, *"EXACTLY. If word gets out about either Eko or Indra, then it is quite possible that one of the other thirty-five teams may draft the other, and for this work, we need both."*

Sheldon was still shocked and simply nodded his head in agreement. Barbara asked, *"Sheldon, are you alright?"*

Finally, Sheldon was able to speak, *"Well, I do want to meet them both immediately. Roger, what do you suggest on how to get these two guys, the twins, drafted?"*

Bill thought for a second and said, *"Well, I can handle the drafting of them both if we keep this to ourselves until the draft is done."* They all agree that, in order for this to work, they will have to keep everything about Eko and

Indra on a need-to-know basis until the Conquistadors draft them.

Sheldon informed Barbara to make arrangements, listing them down, *"Roger, Bill, Ron (the tech guru), DJ (the pitching coach), Mike (the hitters' coach), and a few others including Sheldon to get ready to go and meet Eko and Indra at the Island."* After all, Sheldon wanted to meet them face to face and see them for himself.

Sheldon calls Ron Levy and tells Ron to meet him in his office. As Ron arrives, he introduces Roger and Ron to each other. Sheldon said, *"Ron, I want you to take Roger to your items, the ones that you have been working on, and show him everything."*

"Everything? You sure Sheldon? After all, you said no one but you, Bill, Barbara, or I could see it," Ron confirmed.

Sheldon replies, *"Yes, Ron. Show Roger everything."* While this was happening, Bill was on the phone with the other General Managers to try and make a deal on the upcoming draft for all the teams in the soon-to-happen draft for the final supplemental draft before the pre-season. Bill said after hanging up the phone, *"Sheldon, there's great news!"*

Sheldon asked, *"What is the Great News, Bill?"*

Bill replied, *"Well, we just traded the overall number one pick in the supplemental draft to the Vegas Vipers, and they have agreed to give it to us in exchange for the number one draft pick 38. If we pick number 37, and now number pick 38, we should be able to draft both players back to back. As long as no one is aware of either player."* Upon hearing this, Sheldon exclaimed, *"That's great news, Bill! Good Job! Now go and get ready as we are all going to Indonesia to meet Eko and Indra."*

Ron, by this time, arrived at his lab, where he did the research and development (R&D). His lab was located at the stadium underneath the baseball field. Not many people knew about it, and it had been a well-kept secret during the building of the stadium. Inside the R&D, Ron, with Sheldon's money and backing, had been working on improving the game to bring baseball into the modern era using computers along with technology. This was all to one day improve the game and take the human element of the officiating completely out eventually. It is what they have been working on long before Sheldon became a baseball owner, and before the Albuquerque Conquistadors even existed was this research and development.

They had developed a nanochip that was going to change baseball more than anything since baseball first began. The chips were to be used in all baseballs, bats, gloves, shoes, uniforms, bases, home plate, pitcher's mound, the field, and even throughout the entire fences. The goal was to completely replace the Home Plate umpire and even the officials in the field during all the games.

With technology and computers, and by using these chips combined with the computers would make all pitches the correct call each and every time. Roger asked, *"How is that possible, Ron?"*

"Well, the chips are in the baseballs and the home plate along with the batters uniform and bat. Do you understand that, Roger?"

Upon hearing this, Roger further inquired, *"Yes, I do understand, but how will it work?"*

"When the batter goes to the batter's box, their cleats, the baseball shoes will activate the computer. When the pitcher makes the pitch with the chips in the baseball and

also in home plate, the bat and the induvial batter's uniform will allow the computer to make the right call every time, based on that person's height."

Intrigued by this, Roger replied, *"That is exactly what we will need for our two prospects?"*

Ron asked, confused, *"Who are you talking about, Roger?"*

Before Roger could reply, Ron's cell phone rang. *"Hi, Sheldon. Yes, Sheldon, we are both down here. Really? We are going on a trip, and you want me to bring everything? Ok, great, I will start packing. Bye."*

Ron looked up at Roger and said, *"Looks like we are going on a trip this afternoon, Roger. Sheldon wants you to go to his office, and I need to start packing this stuff up. I finally have a chance to use my equipment and get it all field-tested."*

Chapter 4
The Arrival

Everyone was eagerly waiting at Sheldon's private airfield near Albuquerque to witness the Indonesian giants, Eko and Indra. Sheldon had seen the pictures and taken all the details from Roger, but he was still very nervous. He was only waiting to see them for himself. The Coach DJ, Coach Mike, along with Bernice and Dr. Vegarra, the Conquistadors Head Doctor, were all present to accompany Sheldon for the journey.

A reporter, Susan Vallelunga, with her cameraman, Jeff Ohm, had been invited by Sheldon to tag along to capture and video record these supernatural athletes who were potentially the best that the game had ever seen. Roger, out of everyone there, was calm. However, he still did not like the idea of having reporters on board.

"Do you really think it is a good idea to bring Susan and Jeff here?" Roger asked Sheldon right away.

"Who do you think will market them? And do the paperwork? I have them here for a reason, Roger. Don't worry," Sheldon reasoned back. He had planned

everything and took care of even the minor of the details in planning to do so. He had asked everybody to stay on the Island until the coaches had given clearance of the new athletes, 'Supermen,' as he called them.

Roger advised Sheldon not to refer to them as 'Supermen,' as their names were Eko Suparman and Indra Suparman. He did not want to take up the risk of upsetting them. Idah was to accompany them, and he knew her support was extremely important for things to proceed according to plan.

"You're right, Roger, but to what I have heard and seen, I find them to be like Clark Kent," Sheldon replied with a grin.

"I bet they wouldn't know who Clark Kent is." Roger chuckled and then answered back.

Finally, Ron Levy had arrived. He was there with two semitrailers, which mainly consisted of technological components. The items from the trailers were in the process of being transferred to Sheldon's private jet. He had brought all the equipment that he had been working on for the past decade. He had brought it all because he knew that his gadgets and research had finally found a match.

They were all excited to take off as they had the feeling of being part of something special. Sheldon Winn had managed to build a team. He had a technological expert, the medical staff, and the media team. He was going with complete preparations. The jet had been fully loaded, and they were heading for takeoff. They were to arrive at Jakarta first from where several helicopters were waiting to take them and the equipment to the Island. Roger seemed concerned. He was worried about the two Indonesian boys who were both big and strong from the outside but soft and sensitive from the inside.

He wondered if they would be able to adapt to a new environment. They had never moved outside the Island, let alone Indonesia, and the chances of them being homesick were also to be brought under consideration. Roger had developed a deeper relationship with them because of the time he had spent with them on the Island. He had become their mentor, and their happiness and comfort were equally important to him. He was also curious about Idah's reaction. It was a twelve-hour flight, and Roger had a lot to think about. As soon as they arrived at Jakarta, they shifted from the jet into helicopters.

Ron's modernized equipment had never been tested in the field, and it was to be tested for the first time, which was to be transferred through the helicopters. Without any delay, they set off for the Island of the Suparman brothers. A total of three Helicopters were loaded, and the equipment required two helicopters just to transport the items which they had brought along.

Again, Roger thought about his journey prior to this. It reminded him of the Pilot who saved his life, and he knew that if it wasn't for luck, he wouldn't have been there today making this journey. Had he not boarded that plane, he would have never met Eko and Indra. Luck works in its own way, or was it fate?

"Sit in the co-pilot seat. That way, you can make sure we go to the right place. After all, with over 18,000 Islands, we need to make sure that we go to the right one, Roger." Roger agreed as the first of the three helicopters with passengers was to take off.

Roger spotted the Island and let them know that they were about to arrive. Sheldon asked Roger if he was certain that it was the right one. Roger then pointed at the parachute on a huge boulder that had helped him survive.

He also showed the huge 'S,' which he had made on the sand whilst looking for help. They had all heard the story, and they could all relate to it. Roger directed the pilot to land on a field slightly ahead of the beach. It was the exact field where Roger trained Eko and Indra, who could be seen by everyone in the helicopter from a distance. They were eight feet and eight inches tall, which is why it was hard to miss them.

The villagers were very excited to see Roger, who was noticed after the helicopters landed. He had returned as per his promise. Naturally, Eko and Indra were the first to greet him and were followed by Idah, and then by the rest of the villagers. Sheldon was impressed to see how Roger was welcomed, yet even more impressed at the site of Eko and Indra.

Sheldon and his crew were aware of what they were going to witness. They had seen the pictures and heard of the details from Roger, and yet, when they saw Eko and Indra, they were in a state of shock. To see them live was unreal. They were huge and strong. Roger formally introduced Sheldon and his team to the villagers, to which Idah responded and introduced herself. She also introduced the villagers to the team, and the guests were then all invited to the village to have a feast and spend time together. Ron had not arrived yet. He was left behind to stay and come with the helicopters that had the equipment because the pilots of the helicopters were not employed by Sheldon. They would have leaked the news that he did not want to be disclosed without his approval. The helicopters with the equipment were scheduled to arrive a little later, so the pilots could not know why the team had gone there. There were lots and lots of equipment.

Right after landing, Ron got involved in unloading the equipment. There was no machinery at the village that could be used for unloading them, and so he was not sure how long the unloading was going to take. The pilots were asked to leave the equipment and fly back with the helicopter that had brought the passengers. They were then to wait for the pickup notice.

Ron had calculated everything except the time required to unload the equipment. *"Sorry for the delay, Sheldon, but I still can't tell how long it will take to unload the equipment,"* Ron stated in a confused tone.

"Don't worry, Ron; it'll only take a few minutes." Roger interfered.

"A few minutes?" Ron responded in disbelief.

Roger smiled at him and called Eko and Indra. They had seen the supernatural men, but they had yet not witnessed their uncanny strengths. Roger did tell them what they were capable of, and now they were all going to see it for themselves. From baseball equipment, computers, generators to power computers, they had a lot of items to unload. Ron introduced himself to Eko and Indra and asked them for their help to get the items unloaded.

Ron's mouth was wide open, and he stood in disbelief. He knew the power required to lift the equipment was huge, and he forgot all his math when he saw them do it with ease. Not just Ron, but everybody who had come there with Sheldon was speechless. It actually took them a couple of minutes, where Ron thought it would require a couple of days.

They were indeed extremely powerful. Ron asked them if they could help him in unpacking the sealed containers, which they did without any problem. Ron, who thought would be far behind his schedule, was now far ahead. Eko and Indra were looking at the baseball bats for the very first time. They had been playing baseball ever since they met Roger, but they had never played it with proper equipment with the exception of a baseball. Though Ron had attempted to make them cleats and gloves, they were too small for the two of them. The rest of the equipment was fine. It took a couple of hours to make preparations before the equipment could be tested for the very first time. They were all excited to see them play, and Ron was excited to see his equipment being used. The first thing that he asked them to do was pitch the ball. He set up a radar gun, which told the speed of the pitch when it was released from the pitcher and caught by the catcher.

The radar gun was an improvement of the existing radar guns; it was more precise. The maximum speed the gun could detect was 999 miles per hour. The fastest pitch that had ever been recorded was around 105 miles per hour, which is why Ron was convinced for the speed of 999 miles per hour to be enough to be effective and precise.

The jersey's Eko and Indra were wearing had chips in them, and the baseballs and the home plates had them as well. Ron confirmed the computer was running and signal for the first pitch to be delivered. Since Eko was the elder one, he was to pitch first, and Indra was to catch. Eko immediately released the first pitch. It was so quick that it was impossible to keep track with the naked eye. It was recorded as a strike. The radars were not able to pick the speed, and it left Ron quite surprised. He made the calculations to when the pitch was released and when was it collected. He realized that the radar guns did not have enough speed, and the 999 miles per hour was simply not enough; it certainly needed a fourth digit. That meant that they were able to pitch above 999 miles per hour; it was closer to the speed of bullet over 1,000 miles per hour, a feat never accomplished before today.

Roger was not surprised, and the computers and the equipment confirmed the pitch to be unbelievably accurate. Roger reminded Eko and Indra of the time when he asked Eko to throw a pitch to which they replied that they had already done it. That was when Roger first batted against Indra; they both remembered and smiled at Roger. He asked them to do that again and instructed them as he had earlier that they weren't allowed to do that in a game. They both shook their heads in affirmation.

"Sheldon, Ron, have a look at this?" Roger requested for their attention.

Roger signaled Eko to proceed with the pitch. Ron and Sheldon could not believe what the computers were telling them. The system confirmed three pitches within a second. Sheldon was speechless. He did not have the words to express his disbelief or even appreciate the talent that both Eko and Indra possessed. Again, Ron started doing the math and figured out that the pitcher's speed was somewhere around 1,064 miles per hour. Ron realized that the radar gun indeed required a few changes, and certainly, a fourth digit was to be added.

This continued for a few hours. Eko and Indra kept on rotating their roles of the pitcher and catcher. The display of supernatural skills silenced Sheldon and his team. They watched in admiration, one pitch after another. Roger kept on surprising them; they didn't know what would come next. Roger now asked them to pitch the ball with the other arm.

Coaches, DJ and Mike,said in disbelief at the same time, *"The other arm?"*

Roger replied back, *"Yes, they can pitch with the other arm and have the same accuracy. My question is, does the speed match what Ron figured out?"*

Ron confirmed that the speed of the other arm was equal. And not just the speed, but the accuracy too was remarkably the same. No one in the history of baseball had ever pitched with that speed and accuracy with this consistency. They were all exactly hitting the center with precision. This was not just the case of one of their arms, but both. They then decided to do the base path running test, which would determine their running speed. Ron had designed the cleats which they were to wear for identifying their speed.

Since the cleats were small, they had to come with an alternate plan. Ron suggested that they wrapped their feet with their shirts since their shirts consisted of nanosensors. This way, their speed could be identified and recorded and also tested out Ron's equipment. Every time he touched the base, the computer was to determine their speed. The computer displayed their running speed to be around 364 miles per hour.

They ran across all the bases from first base back to Home Plate within a second. Since the running speed was within the radar gun's range; it would be able to identify the true running speed of both Eko and Indra. Ron decided to use the radar gun, which confirmed the speed to be 364 miles per hour, which was insanely quick. They were quicker on foot than a sports car was on wheels! Sheldon had an easy call to make. He went to Roger and confirmed to him that he could keep the remaining two Million dollars as per the agreement.

"You can have the five million, Roger. I will surely pay the two of them handsomely," he said.

"So, Sheldon, how does it feel to be making billions by the end of the season?" Roger replied, indicating towards him to have the maximum gain out of the deal.

"It's a long way to go. There's a lot of paperwork that has to be taken care of. There might be challenges which might be hidden right now. Let's hope it all works out." Sheldon ended the discussion before it even started.

The sun was about to set, and it was about to get dark. Idah invited everybody for dinner, and since she was the leader of the village, they agreed and started to pack up to return to the village. On the way back, Dr. Vegarra approached Sheldon.

He raised up a point that Sheldon had missed. *"They can be dangerous, Sheldon. People can die if hit by their strikes,"* he said. He had a valid point; he was not certain to what security and safety measures were to be taken as it was a serious issue. Sheldon agreed. They had to keep the fans and opposing players safe at all costs. They hadn't batted yet, and their batting could be even more harmful. Arrangements were to be made, which included upgrades in the stadium according to what Dr. Vegarra recommended. It had gotten dark, and everybody was in the village. As per tradition, the villagers had a storytime after dinner.

Bernice had planned something special with Sheldon; she had decided to distribute gifts among the villagers since they had been very hospitable. Bernice thought that it was best if they appreciated their hospitality. Every villager was gifted with multiple items, which also included hats, shirts, and other accessories with Sheldon's club's name on it. Idah and the villagers were very appreciative of the efforts made by the owner of the Conquistadors.

While the guests and the villagers were enjoying dinner and exchanging gifts, Eko and Indra were busy assembling huts for the guests to sleep. They gathered materials that were required to build huts and assembled them without taking much time. Roger, Idah, Sheldon, and Bernice then took a stroll along the beach. It was a beautiful night with a sky full of millions and millions of stars.

"So, Roger and Sheldon, I want you to know that we, as in Eko, Indra, the villagers, and myself, have agreed to let Eko and Indra go with you to play baseball. Yet, I too will be coming with them," Idah said while gazing at the stars, then the water, and finally at the three of them.

Idah was a very calm woman and a very soft-spoken one. They were never going to have any problem in taking her along. Roger and Sheldon agreed without a moment's pause. It was as if they had made her mind that she was coming with them before she even spoke about it.

They further discussed how they were to be moved from Indonesia to the States. Bernice informed them that Sheldon was to leave in the morning since he had a lot of work pending. Sheldon was to be accompanied by the coaches, while the doctor, cameraman, Bernice, and Roger were all to stay at the village with Idah and the two boys.

Idah asked Sheldon straight away this time while looking at nobody but the water, *"why are you leaving so soon, Sheldon? Can't you stay for a few more days?"*

"There is a lot of work to be done, and in order to get you guys there on time as I have promised, I'll have to go there and start working. I wish I could have stayed longer, but I can't," he replied in a comforting tone. After a long walk across the shore, they headed back towards the village. On returning, Sheldon informed his team about his decision to return in the morning.

Sheldon then found Susan and Jeff and instructed them, *"I want you to film everything and anything while I am gone. Keep everything tight, and by 'no' means no exposure or any leak to the outside world until you hear directly from me. After we draft Eko and Indra, you two will have the exclusives and also be the only reporter to have access to them. This is going to be huge!"*

Sheldon picked up his satellite phone and made a conference call to Barbara and Bill, who were still back in Albuquerque. He told them that he needed a helicopter in exactly six hours. He also asked them to ensure that the other pilots tagged along as he needed all the helicopters gone from the village.

He indicated that a few changes were to be made, but did not get much into the details. Barbara confirmed that she would contact the pilot in Jakarta and make all the necessary arrangements for his return. It would require him twenty hours to get back, and they agreed on discussing Roger's discovery on his return. Sheldon, before hanging up, lost control over his excitement and said, *"It is a billion times better than I could have expected or hoped. Roger did indeed find us, two superstars, that…Barbara, I haven't even seen them bat yet, and with the pitching alone, they certainly will make us the overall favorites to win the World Series in year one."*

"That is wonderful news! I will see you when you get back. Sheldon, call me if you need anything. Goodnight." Barbara responded.

"Goodnight, Barbara."

The next morning, Sheldon hadn't slept at all and was still wide awake. He decided that, prior to the helicopter's arrival, he wanted to see both Eko and Indra do some hitting. Eko and Indra were more than willing, and just before the Sun was beginning to rise, Eko, Indra, Roger, Sheldon, Ron, Coach DJ, and Coach Mike all went to the practice field.

As per usual, the first to bat was Eko, and that too, with an official bat. It looked like a pen would in an adult's hand. Eko batted from the left side of the batter's box as a lefty. DJ threw a pitch that Eko blasted with the flick of his right-hand wrist. The ball went soaring so far that they couldn't even see where it landed. It was definitely headed towards the ocean. Instantly, Indra, within a few moments, retrieved the wet baseball from the ocean.

Sheldon suggested, *"Indra, you or Eko don't have to get those baseballs, we have a few hundreds of them here."*

Indra replied, *"I like to have the baseballs; besides, they fall apart after a few hits, and we need all that we can have while you're leaving, Sheldon."*

They were both very strong and hit the ball with only their wrist. Just like pitching, they could hit the ball from both sides. The balls were hit so hard that they could not last for more than a few hits. Sheldon realized the point that Dr. Vagerra made regarding how safety was extremely important to be brought into consideration. He also thought that the umpires were not capable of seeing the pitches, and Ron's inventions were to be integrated into the game if Eko and Indra were to play.

The helicopters were soon to arrive, which is why Sheldon had decided to return to the village from the practice field. On his way back, he asked Roger to keep Eko and Indra away from the sight of the pilots. He knew that if the news leaked, and that they had found out about the two of them before the draft was completed, then there could be complications which might even result in closing down their chance of easily securing the twins if Eko and Indra were to play for the Conquistadors. Roger could only agree.

Chapter 5
The Draft And Modernization Of Baseball

It had been over two weeks since Sheldon had left the Island. Along with Bill, he was preparing the official supplemental draft, which was to have six expansion teams drafting for the top six spots. The existing thirty teams were to follow based on their performance in the previous season. The teams were to be arranged on the basis of worst to best, which meant that the teams with the worst performance were to be on the lower side of the table.

Prior to the supplemental draft, the Conquistadors agreed with the Vegas Vipers to have two drafts picked in a row. They were to draft in positions picking 'pick 37' and 'pick 38' simultaneously. All the teams were present, and the drafting had begun as per schedule. There was a bit of confusion looking at how the odds had dropped on Conquistadors to win the World Series. Also, the fact that the Conquistadors had given up all the numbers to draft at #38 lead to many speculations.

Though there were all sorts of rumors, none of them knew who Sheldon was planning to introduce. All the baseball executives, general managers, and fans were wondering what Sheldon and the Conquistadors had in store. They had drafted for players who had no past experience and weren't even a part of any clubs prior to the Conquistadors. No matter how talented the bottom tier players were to be, to have them directly in the World Series did not seem sensible at all. This was the first phase which had made the crowd excited. Bill wondered how they would react when they would actually see who the new players were and what they were capable of.

The first round had ended, and the second round was about to begin. Sheldon was starting to get nervous as he just wanted to get done with the entire process and directly jump on to game day. He was constantly shaking his right leg, and his eyes were focusing at a point indicating that he was lost in deep thoughts. Barbara, sitting alongside, had noticed his nervousness and held his hand to calm him down. As soon as she grabbed his hand, it seemed like he was pulled out of his dreams back into reality.

Every minute seemed longer than ever. Finally, it was time for their pick to be announced, and so did the baseball commissioner.

"With Pick #37, the Albuquerque Conquistadors select EKO SUPARMAN."

The voices had gotten louder, and a discussion broke out amongst the audience as to who Eko was. The baseball commissioner continued without any further delay towards the next pick, which was again of the Conquistadors. *"With Pick #38, the Albuquerque Conquistadors select ...INDRA SUPARMAN."*

The noise in the crowd had increased, and everyone in the crowd was talking about the Suparman brothers. It was like every person in the crowd was discussing Sheldon's picks, and he could hear all the speculations quite clearly now.

"Never heard of them, what a waste to give up the number one pick for players that no one has heard of or even knows about." Sheldon heard one of the team managers say.

He secretly smiled at it while trying to maintain a poker face.

"We will all know very soon if it is or isn't a waste," he thought to himself. It was the joke of the evening to have Conquistadors have two picks, which no one knew about. The media had no mercy on the team and their pick, and despite having no information about who the Suparman brothers were, the news was all over the T.V and baseball magazines. It wasn't just the media, but baseball officials of every club that were to be a part of Major League Baseball found it hilarious as they considered that the Conquistadors were either giving up or had an incompetent management team. The discussion when on from late-night television shows to headlines.

The Suparman brothers were talked about everywhere. Though Sheldon was expecting them to be all over the news once they got there, he had not expected that before they were known. But he was enjoying the reactions because he knew that they were all going to be blown away once they saw who the Eko and Indra were. The fans in Albuquerque were very disappointed and demanded refunds for the tickets that they had purchased. They were hoping to see the Conquistadors pick a star player instead of picking players nobody knew about. Sheldon, Bill, and Barbara were calm and happy. They knew such reactions were to be expected from the fans were just like the rest; they weren't aware of the players that they were about to bring as well. They celebrated their picks. They finally had the rights and had drafted both Eko and Indra successfully. Sheldon immediately contacted Roger and informed him about the completion of the draft. Eko and Indra were to join the rest of the team in Albuquerque and leave with Roger in a couple of days. Everything was going as per the plan, and they had accomplished what they wanted with much ease. Meanwhile, the media had surrounded Sheldon and his team trying to know anything about the players, or at least the reason behind going for inexperienced ones.

"In due time, you and the rest of the world will learn firsthand of Eko and Indra. We are just blessed to have such fine players for our team," was all they would reply with to every single question thrown their way.

They gave no information to anyone and focused on making all the necessary arrangements for their arrival. Now, it was time for the second official meeting. The Commissioner of Major League Baseball had a similar reaction, only that he had made efforts to make this league a success, which he thought was being ruined by Sheldon. He wanted the teams to be competent and had an urge to win rather than to draw away the fans' interest by picking incompetent players. Sheldon and Bill were persistent and somehow managed to convince the commissioner about their intentions of winning. They were finally allowed to be a part of the owner's meetings, which were to be held in New York. It was not just the commissioner who thought so, but owners of most of the clubs had a similar perception about Conquistadors and Sheldon. They had all invested a lot on their teams and did not want it to be ruined because of one owner. All of the clubs were looking forward to the meeting. Firstly, because it was going to take them a step closer to the start of the league, and secondly, they wanted to know what Sheldon was up to.

Some of them were already in New York while others had to get there. All of them had one concern in common, which was the Conquistador's picks. The meeting started at the given time, and all the owners had ensured their availability. The Commissioner started with the brief regarding the opening in which he bluntly criticized Sheldon. He had agreed earlier that he would allow Sheldon to speak in his defense, and his team was only to be permitted to be a part of the league if he was able to convince the Commissioner and the owners.

Sheldon was asked to proceed to the podium and reason with the crowd regarding his selections. He looked at all the owners who were all looking at him. It was pin-drop silence, which was to be broken by Sheldon's speech. *"Everyone, first off, thanks for allowing me to be here. I know that most of you have reservations related to my intent, which I hope will all go away when I leave this meeting. I have two things that I plan on presenting. First of those two things is the need for upgrades and integration of technology that will take this game to a whole new level. It is time for us to no longer have umpires, but rather use technology that we have created to make baseball as fair as possible. It will lead to creating a perfect system."*

The crowd did not like what he was saying, and the reactions were not at all pleasant. Sheldon continued ignoring the moans. *"We have perfected a system that will call every single pitch both correctly and fairly with 100% accuracy for every pitch. This will be done by taking out the human element and is something I know a lot of you owners and most fans have wanted. This upcoming season will require that all stadiums... yes, all stadiums, including ours in Albuquerque, is upgraded for fan safety to ensure no serious injuries or worse."*

The crowd still seemed unconvinced, and one of the owners interfered, *"What are you trying to sell us, Sheldon?"*

Sheldon once again ignored the comment and resumed, *"I am very serious, for when we play against any of your teams, you could be liable if you do not make these changes immediately. And besides, shouldn't today's technology be used to keep things fair and honest? Does anyone agree with me on that?"*

More than half of the audience shook their heads in agreement. Another owner shouted out, *"Tell me why we need to ensure the safety of our fans when we play you at our stadium?"*

Sheldon gave Barbara the signal, and she left her seat approaching the projector. Without much delay, she played the video. It opened up with Sheldon on an Island with Susan Vallelunga, the reporter who most of the crowd recognized.

"Hi, Everyone! This is Susan Vallelunga here in one of the 18,000 plus islands of Indonesia with Sheldon Wynn,

the billionaire and now owner of the Expansion Baseball Team, the Albuquerque Conquistadors. We are out here because of a former scout, Roger Schafer, who, while out here, was involved in a plane crash. Roger was forced out of an airplane and happened to land on this island by sheer chance. While Roger was here, he was found by two twin brothers. These twin brothers are Eko Suparman and Indra Suparman, and they are often called the Superman Twins. You will soon learn why they have been called 'Supermen,' and it's not just because of their surnames.

However, unlike any other twins, they are eight feet eight inches tall, and they can run up to 364 miles per hour. Yes, you heard me correctly; THEY CAN RUN UP TO 364 MILES PER HOUR EACH. On a baseball field using standard baseball regulations, they can leave the home plate, touch every single base, and be back at home plate in less than a second."

The footage then showed a clip of them doing it.

"If you think that is amazing then get this, they can both pitch, and when I say pitch, their pitches are at 1,064 miles per hour with perfect accuracy. They pitch so fast that the human eye can't even see or follow it."

Again the video feed displayed their capability.

"What's even more amazing is that they can pitch using either arm and from what I have seen personally, they do not ever slow down or get tired. And again 1,064 miles per hour, no umpire can even see the pitches, and no batter will be able even to swing it in time. This is what Sheldon has picked.

First, up will be Eko; he is the older of the two twins and will bat first."

The video showed Eko batting using one hand and how the bat looked like a pen in his hand. As soon as the pitch approached Eko, he, with a single-hand wrist flick, blasted the ball so far and so fast that the camera is unable to show where it landed.

"Believe me, everyone watching this, these are all true, and yes, they will be playing for Conquistadors this upcoming season."

The last part of the video had Susan directly addressing the viewers.

"What Sheldon is proposing to you is absolutely true. You MUST make changes in your stadiums to ensure the safety of your fans when they are batting. If this force doesn't kill a person, it could cause lifelong serious injuries, and you, as the owner, would be surrounded by lawsuits."

The video silenced the crowd, and they were in a state of disbelief. What they had witnessed was unnatural, and everything Sheldon had said started to make sense. *"How can we even compete with that?"* one owner exclaimed.

"They are going to win the World Series." Another owner stated its agreement. Not a single owner seemed calm as they could all see their chances of winning the World Series disappear.

The Commissioner, who, at first, had expressed great disappointment was speechless. After taking a decent pause, he asked Sheldon, *"Sheldon, is this real?"*

Sheldon replied, *"Yes, Sir, and this is why we need to have the game modernized. After all, you can't even see their pitches, and we will all, as owners, have to make the necessary upgrades to protect our fans."*

The owner of Louisiana Nobles asked, *"How are we going to do that?"*

Sheldon then was ready to surprise them even more. He showed them what Ron had designed. The screen now had an image of a net-like structure that seemed solid yet transparent. *"We call this Adamantium Vibrium. We came up with this name from the comic books. This mesh is lightweight and can be installed all around the open seats to ensure the safety of the fans. We have created it, we have tested it, and it does work. The best thing about it is that it doesn't block or change the fan's viewpoint as netting does. It is simple to install, and we have begun its production to ensure all stadiums have it before the Suparman brothers start playing."*

Another owner moaned, *"At what cost do you plan on selling it, how much are you going to make out of it?"*

Sheldon replied in a firm voice, *"You don't have to pay me anything. We will bear the cost of installation. Now, before you ask why we are not making profits from it... The reason is that we expect our fan merchandise to be sold ten times more with Eko and Indra on board. We will profit that way through our merchandise. So yes, it will be on us. We have it already installed at our ballpark along with the automated modernization."*

"What is modernization?" Sheldon is asked by the owner of the North Carolina team.

He responded, *"Let me have Ron Levy, our developer, explain that to you. Ron, would you please come on up?"*

Ron stood up from his seat and went to the podium.

He took the microphone from Sheldon and began to speak, *"Hello Everyone. My name is Ron Levy, believe it or not, Sheldon and I began this nearly fifteen years ago. It was a long time before the expansion happened, and we both wanted to see baseball improve. Yes, both of us are, and always will be, baseball fans first and love baseball long before Sheldon was an owner. Like most of you, and certainly like the majority of our fans, our biggest issue with baseball has been the human aspect of the sport, especially the home plate umpire and officials.*

How many times have you seen an umpire not call strikes, strikes? How many times have batters, pitchers, players, coaches, and even fans complained about that alone? I know that I have done so many times while watching a game on T.V or a stadium. So way back then, we began creating a system to not only improve but also make it fair and get the right decision each and every time. We have done that and tested its operations.

We decided that, if we are to replace the home plate umpire, what about the other officials and the calls they made. So we took care of that too by using today's technology and using nanochips. The nanochips are put in everything, and when I say everything, I mean everything. That includes uniforms for individual players, strike zones, baseball bats. When they cross the plate and say they didn't, the difficult calls are no more dependent on the judgment capability of a human. Rather, when the ball is caught, for example, at first base, then the ball that has nanochips as does the first baseman's glove and cleats.

So if the ball is caught and the cleat is not touching the first base, then the runner is out. Just like it would work in reverse for the runner. If the runner touches the base prior to the ball being caught, he is safe. And this is for every base, and every call, including foul balls, infield fly rules, and questionable home runs in fair or foul territory. We have covered it all, and it functions with a 100% accuracy."

Ron then handed the microphone back to Sheldon and walked back towards his seat. Sheldon then regained the attention of the officials seated and said, *"Isn't this how baseball should be? Isn't this what, for decades, fans and players have wanted, and isn't it time we did this?"*

The commissioner raised his hand to which Sheldon chuckled, *'Yes, Mr. Commissioner?"*

The commissioner stated, *"I like it. And yes, as a fan, this is something that we do need, and I believe it will indeed change the game for the better. After all, making the right call is of utmost importance as a fan and a person that is a lifelong baseball lover. And since you claim it to be functional and tested, I don't think a lot of us might disagree either."*

Since all the owners and their representatives were present, the commissioner decided to take a vote on the issue of implementing these technologies. All the owners, except one, voted in favor of the implementation. The owner that didn't agree was concerned that the Umpires and other officials who would have their Labor Unions fight this modernization as they were to lose their jobs if these changes were made.

Though the human resources required were going to be replaced by computers and nanotechnology, the game was to change unlike anything ever before. It was thirty-five votes in support and just one against the changes. That meant that these changes were to be made effective.

Since Eko and Indra were being introduced in the sport, there wasn't much of an option to go against the changes as the safety of the fans had to be taken care of. Every team had to play against Albuquerque Conquistadors, and they had to make sure necessary measures were taken. All the equipment, uniforms and baseball fields were to be modified by using the technological advancements before the first game of the season. This season was to be the fairest season yet played, and that fairness could only be achieved by modernization.

Sure, umpires and other officials would lose jobs in the process, yet thousands would be hired to replace them and also would require a human official in the announcer's box for any calls that were challenged or may be questioned. This would keep the officials union somewhat happy knowing that they would still have a place in baseball.

Chapter 6
Albuquerque Conquistadors Official Team Roster

Now that the Albuquerque Conquistadors had indeed drafted Eko and Indra, all that was required was to sign them to the contracts. Roger Schafer happened to have been recently approved after he was *"Fired"* by Sheldon and was the Agent that would be representing both Eko and Indra Suparman. Roger became rather excited upon hearing the news that the draft did indeed happen as everyone hoped and expected.

Roger announced to everyone on the Island, *"Everyone, please gather around, I have news that I want to share with everyone."* The guests and villagers surrounded Roger as he stated, *"Great news, everyone! Eko and Indra are both official members of the Albuquerque Conquistadors, as we all hoped and wanted. Everyone on the tribe can join us in New Mexico if they want, with Idah, Eko, Indra, and Myself."*

Being a small village of fifty-one people, Roger figured that it would be best to bring everyone. Hopefully, if they did want to come all that way, then Eko and Indra couldn't possibly become homesick. After all, each and everyone in the tribe was family, maybe not by blood yet by bonds. Some of the villagers certainly wanted to go, and a few of them were not certain if they wanted to go too.

Eko, Indra, and Idah were certainly happy with this announcement by Roger. Even though Roger didn't have Sheldon's permission, he knew that, by doing this, it would create a better situation for the twins. After all, as the agent, he knew that whatever deal would be made, he would have enough money to take care of each and every one of the tribal members. After all, you can't bring baseball to the island in a professional way, yet you can bring the Villagers to Albuquerque.

It was finally agreed at supper that night that everyone would be making the journey together as a family and to support both Eko and Indra. Sheldon, of course, had no idea that this was happening. When Sheldon checked in with Susan Vallelunga, the reporter on one of their calls, Susan informed Sheldon of Roger's proposal.

Sheldon was not too happy for that, yet when Sheldon spoke with Barbara Sue about this, she instantly agreed what Roger had done was for the best. Now, the concern was, how would they get all fifty-one villagers the Passports in such a short time frame?

Sheldon had already made arrangements for Eko, Indra, and even Idah with immigration to ensure that the twins would be available for the first game of the opening season.

Barbara, being Barbara, was able to change Sheldon's thought after hearing her reasonable and factual comment, which was, *"This would indeed be best for Eko and Indra. Hopefully, it would also limit any chances of getting homesick and not wanting to finish the season, or worse, become so homesick that they quit the team altogether."*

Barbara was then requested by Sheldon to make contact with the President of the United States to help ensure that this could be done in a timely matter. It included everyone in the entire village. After all, even though Sheldon himself was a powerful and well-respected man, even his power was limited by the immigration offices. He knew that this would be the best and fastest way to ensure that everyone would be able to come together. Back on the Island, everyone was very excited because this would, indeed, be the first time for many of the younger villagers to leave the island, including both Eko and Indra. Some of the older members of the tribe did, at one time or another, live elsewhere before they ended up on the Island. However, none of them except for Idah has ever been to the United States of America.

Most of them knew nothing about life or what America was like because they had always lived a simple life, and without any technology such as television, movies, radio, internet, they lived their lives day by day. Roger was speaking to everyone about how things were much more different in America, and that at least by going to Albuquerque, New Mexico, they would certainly have a much slower lifestyle. After all, the Albuquerque area was much smaller than most of the other cities where Major League Baseball was played. Roger's phone rang, and he answered, *"Hello, this is Roger."*

Sheldon was on the other end of the phone saying, *"Roger, I was informed that you invited the entire tribe to join Eko, Indra, and Idah as well. Is that correct?"*

Roger replied, *"Yes, Sheldon. I did, and everyone is excited to go."*

Sheldon responded, *"Well, Roger, this will change our plans. We can't have everyone come as we expected, at least not on the schedule that we had. Barbara has been speaking to the United States President, and together, they are trying to expedite the paperwork of the passports for everyone.*

This is going to take some time. However, Barbara suggested that everyone should get ready to go and be transported to my jet. Then they could leave Jakarta and go to St. Thomas to my estate. After all, St. Thomas will not require passports, and this will be a way to help them all adjust to life outside of their village."

Roger fully agreed, and it was decided that the entire group, including all the other villagers, would get ready to leave the next day via helicopter to the airport in Jarkata. Once in Jarkata, they would all go to the private airstrip where one of Sheldon's jets would be waiting to fly them to St. Thomas and go to Sheldon's resort.

With the regular season now three weeks away from the opening, changing things would mean that there were more chances that Eko and Indra wouldn't even be in Albuquerque until a couple of days before the opening game. This would leave little to no time for the other players on the Conquistadors, and also Eko and Indra a chance to get to know each other. Sheldon was not concerned with this; however, Roger certainly was. But the good thing was that this would allow Sheldon the time to make arrangements for the entire village to be found a place to call home.

When Sheldon mentioned this, Roger responded, *"I think that the best thing would be a place small enough with not too many people. After all, Eko and Indra will be sought out by the media and press, unlike anything either of us has ever seen. Someplace low key would be best, and of course, limited to actually know where they reside."*

Sheldon agreed and stated that the perfect place would be on the outskirts of Santa Fe, New Mexico. It was very small in population and a far slower-paced place than Albuquerque was.

Just as Sheldon and Roger finished their conversation, Barbara entered Sheldon's office and stated, *"Sheldon, turn on your Television. It doesn't matter which channel, just turn it on."* Sheldon grabbed the remote control and turned on the television. Immediately, there was footage of the owners meeting in New York earlier, which had been leaked and was now showing on every channel. Sheldon then looked at Barbara, smiling and very happy. Within a few minutes, all of their lines were ringing nonstop. Yes, they had officially been discovered by the News and Media, and everyone was interested in the Conquistador's newest players, Eko and Indra Suparman. Barbara's cell phone rang, and the caller was the President of the United States.

He started, *"Hello, Barbara. This is the President. Is there any chance that Sheldon is around?"*

Excitedly, Barbara handed her cell phone to Sheldon. *"Sheldon! It's the President of the United States, and he wishes to speak to you!"*

Immediately, Sheldon grabbed the phone and said, *"Hello, Mr. President. This is Sheldon Winn. How are you, sir?"*

After a few moments, when their conversation was complete, and Sheldon handed the phone back to Barbara.

Barbara said, *"So, what did the President of the United States want with You?"*

Sheldon replied, *"He informed me that they are working on getting everyone approved from the Island. He also asked if what he is seeing is true, to which I informed him that it is. And I also told him that it is even far more impressive in real life. Then Mr. President asked me if it was at all possible to be allowed on the Games on Opening Weekend when we play the Dodgers. And I said yes."* Barbara smiled and nodded her head in approval.

Sheldon then informed Barbara, *"Barbara, please inform our players and family members on the Island that we have another change of plans. They will not be going to St. Thomas, but they will be going to Washington, D.C. There, you and I will be meeting them with the President of the United States in order to get them all the legal paperwork to allow them to stay and live in the USA."* During the entire time, the phones continue to ring non-stop.

The head Coach, Benjamin Chaves, was home sleeping and woke to the ringing of his phone. Bill Bell, the General Manager, was calling Coach Chaves, *"Good Morning*

Coach Chaves, this is Bill Bell. I am calling you and need you to gather up the entire team, all the players, family members of the players, coaches, and their families. We are all going to Washington, D.C., in one of Sheldon's jets to meet the President and your new players."

This made the Coach sit up as he asked, *"Finally, I get to see our two supermen?"*

To this, Bill replied, *"Yes, you do. Oh, and you're all going to meet the President."*

Flabbergasted, Coach Chaves said, *"The President?"*

Bill replied, *"Yes, Coach. The President. As in the President of the United States. Start making the calls; everyone needs to be at Sheldon's private airport in five hours."*

Roger, Idah, Eko, Indra, and everyone else was still unaware of the changes as they were all loading up in the helicopters to be taken to the airport where Sheldon's jet was waiting. Finally, they were informed, just as the last helicopter was lifting off the island that had been home to Eko and Indra since they were infants. Some of the villagers were becoming air sick, for none of them had ever flown before. Yet, Eko and Indra loved this. Even with the tight spaces and discomfort. After all, not too many eight foot eight inch tall people were taken into consideration for comfort on a helicopter. But that didn't stop them from the sheer joy of that first flight. All of the villagers looked out as their island became smaller and smaller as the helicopters made their way towards Jarkata. As they finally arrived, the news spread about how Eko and Indra were in the City. By this time, everyone worldwide with any source to television, radio, internet, or even print media was now aware of the twins. It was shown quite often on every single channel and various broadcasts. Quite often, there came people who believed this to be some type of hoax. After all, why would they have not heard of these two young men before now?

However, more often than not, there were many others who did believe but yet wanted more. They wanted to know more, to learn more, and to see more of Eko and Indra. Within a matter of hours since the broadcast, the most often searched entry of the day was Eko and Indra. However, the only thing which was known was that of the leaked film, which the Conquistadors presented at the Owners meeting.

That, in itself, urged the media to find out more about these two supermen. Sheldon, Sheldon's staff, Coaches, Players, and the families were heading to the Airfield where Sheldon's jets were, and it was packed for miles and miles. It was not just the media, but there were also people lined up. Hundreds of thousands of people were lined up thinking that Eko and Indra were already in Albuquerque now.

Now the team's bus and all the other busses were on the way to the Jet. Sheldon and everyone else was amazed and couldn't put into words what they were seeing or experiencing. Barbara was sitting next to Sheldon and said, *"Well, Sheldon, I think you will not have to worry about having too many seats empty during our games this year."*

Smiling back, Sheldon responded with, *"Barbara, this is going to be far better than even I expected or hoped. We are indeed living the dream. I hope that this is a sign of what's to come."*

Barbara nodded her head. After a nearly two hour delay, the Conquistadors were finally at the airport and would soon be leaving Albuquerque, New Mexico, with the next stop being Washington, D.C. to meet Eko, Indra, and even the President of the United States. There were a total of twenty-three players, twelve coaches, Sheldon, and his group is another fourteen, along with their spouses and children.

A total of 124 passengers were finally in the air en route Washington, D.C., where this would be the first time that the majority of these people would meet both Eko and Indra. When the Conquistadors jet finally arrived in Washington D.C., the passengers on Sheldon's Jet could see from the sky before they even reached that a huge mass of people was crowded at the airport. There were possibly hundreds of thousands of people. It was a sight, unlike anything seen before today. For the Eko and Indra, the fever was growing larger and larger by each passing minute. Like the people in New Mexico, everyone present at the Airport near Washington, D.C. believed that both Eko and Indra were with the others arriving.

However, Eko, Indra, Idah, Roger, and everyone else was still nearly four hours away. Roger had an idea of what was happening, but yet, by no means did he know how large these gatherings were. During the flight, Susan Vallelunga and her trusty cameraman, Jeff Ohm, had been busy making documentaries about Eko and Indra with both of the twins and also the other villagers from the tribe.

After all, the marketing of the Conquistadors had exceeded any reasonable expectation by a million times over. Yet, none of them had any idea that this was, without a doubt, the biggest event of any of their lives. As the Jet was a few minutes away from finally arriving with Eko and Indra, they would soon be at the Nation's Capital and would be meeting the world's most powerful person: the President of the United States.

However, to both Eko and Indra, they had no concept of what that would even mean. To Eko, Indra, and the rest of the tribe, he would just be another person. As the jet finally landed on the tarmac, Eko and Indra's other teammates on the Conquistadors were at hand to meet and greet them. Only this time, the President, along with Sheldon, Barbara, and the President's Secret Service, was present with the others.

This would be the first time that they all will see and meet both Eko and Indra. It was, indeed, a long journey since they left the Island. As they begin to depart the jet, Roger was the first to step out. He noticed Sheldon and saw that he was with the President, which is a surprise that he did not expect.

Then finally, Eko being the eldest, was the first to duck under the door hatch, followed by Indra. It only took a few moments before the crowd made any noise. At first, everyone was silent, and their mouths were wide open. Then, all of a sudden, one of the player's small daughter said,*" It is Eko and Indra.....Hi Eko and Indra!"*

Then everyone in attendance cheered, they made enough noise that the others in or even near the airport heard the cheering. For now, they had officially landed in the United States of America and were the most recognized people on the entire planet, but were completely unaware of any of this. In less than a second after spotting Sheldon, both Eko and Indra were seen standing by him. Even the President's Secret Service wasn't able to stop them, for they moved too fast even to react. By the time they realized what happened, one of the Secret Service Agents had her gun pointing at Indra. She tells Indra,*"You, err...both you move away from the President."*

The President then steps in directly in the line of fire and tells the agent, *"Put your gun down, immediately. No one is to pull any of their guns out, and no one is to point a loaded weapon at either of my two guests."*

Sheldon then immediately went and thanked the President. After meeting him, both Eko and Indra are happy to see the teammates and their families. Both of them were overjoyed to meet their teammates and especially their children. All the children were drawn to the two brothers, just as the two brothers were drawn to them. Then the villager's children joined in as they finally departed the Jet.

Roger had a tear, and Idah asked, *"Why do you cry, Roger?"*

To this, Roger wiped the tear and replied, *"Idah, these are tears of joy, for it is so wonderful to see not only Eko and Indra but to see them and all the children being so happy and having a wonderful time. This is far better than what I could ever hope or dream of."*

Idah responded to Roger, saying, *"This is your family now. It is our family, Roger, and we are all one family now."* After the meeting and spending a few hours at the airport, the crowds outside had grown so large that hundreds of thousands of people were lining the streets where they would soon depart. Even the air space outside the airport had several hundred helicopters from various media hoovering in the air.

The crowds were so large that the President of the United States had his security detail call in for additional help to ensure that they would be able to leave the airport and head to 1600 Pennsylvania. That was the address of the White House and where the President lived. Normally, the trip would be about 30-40 minutes, but because of the sheer numbers of people, the trip took nearly three hours to arrive at the White House.

Everyone at the White House was shocked to see Eko and Indra are shocked. To see these two nineteen-year-old twins that stood eight feet and eight inches tall was a sight to see. More and more leaked footage was being seen by others outside of the White House. After a few hours, everyone from the tribe, all fifty-one of them, were then legally provided Green Cards and had been approved to be in the United States legally.

With the season soon to start, it was now time for them to leave Washington D.C. and head back to Albuquerque to begin the next chapter as Conquistadors Baseball players.

Chapter 7
Life In New Mexico

Because of the crowds which Eko and Indra had created, it was decided and suggested by the President and agreed by Sheldon that the planes would not land at Sheldon's Private Airfield. Rather, because of the President's suggestion, they would now land at Kirkland Air Force base because it was much more secure, and the public wasn't allowed access unless approved in advance. As the first of the two of Sheldon's jets landed, the fever, even at Kirkland Air Force base, was very high.

For it was official that Eko, Indra, the villagers, and the entire team would soon be in Albuquerque. The second that the jet landed, the first jet passengers departed the plane except for the players, coaches, and both Eko and Indra. Prior to leaving Washington, D.C., Coach Chaves discussed with Sheldon that it might be good for the other players on the team and also the coaches to get to know both Eko and Indra, and also for Eko and Indra to get to know their new teammates and coaches. As the second jet was now allowing those passengers to depart, the first to exit Eko followed by Indra. The members and staff of the

Airforce Base in Attendance, like everyone else who saw Eko and Indra for the first time, were shocked. They saw both twins for a second, and yet, they seemed to disappear right before their own eyes because of the ability to run at 364 miles per hour.

Then, out of nowhere, all of the people in attendance were cheering them both, screaming, *"Welcome Eko and Indra!"* Idah was very happy to see how much joy that both Eko and Indra were bringing complete strangers. She turned to Roger and said, *"Roger, this is a good thing. All of these people are here because of Eko and Indra and are happy."*

Roger then turned to Idah and replied, *"Yes, Idah, not only here but from what I am learning, this is how the entire world thinks of Eko and Indra."*

Because the crowd outside the base was growing by the passing second, they decided that it would be best for Eko, Indra, Idah, Roger, and the other forty-eight villagers to leave the base via helicopters and go to what would be their home for and during the upcoming baseball season. It was a place just North of Santa Fe where Barbara found and purchased for the entire Villagers along with Eko, Indra, Idah, and Roger to call home.

The players, coaches, and people from the management were loading on to the transportation to take them back to the ballpark from the air force base. Most of the people who were waiting to see both Eko and Indra had no idea that they had just left on a helicopter to see their new home just outside of Santa Fe. Hundreds of thousands of people from the base to the ballpark were lined in the streets waiting to see for themselves both Eko and Indra. Yet, unaware they are not even on one of the vehicles.

It took those going to the baseball field nearly three hours longer than the helicopter flight, which was just outside of Santa Fe to arrive. The first of four helicopters arrived on the estate, where they were met by the employees hired to do the housekeeping, cook meals, transport, and security.

Sheldon knew that the security would have to be that of what the President of the United States had. They were all on a tour of the estate, which was 300 acres with forty homes on the site for the new residents and the staff. Upon the completion of the tour, they were then allowed to choose which homes were not currently occupied by the staff for the time being. Sheldon had Barbara Sue spare no expense in making sure that the new home would be beneficial to everyone in the entire tribe. After several long trips and many hours of traveling, everyone had decided that now was the time to go and get some good rest finally. Back in Albuquerque, at this time, the transportation was finally entering into the stadium. All the changes that were made had finally been completed, and the ballpark was now ready for the season to begin. It had been a long two days for everyone in the group, and just outside the secured area, thousands and thousands of fans were waiting and hoping to get a chance to see both Eko and Indra. Even the airplanes and helicopters were everywhere in the sky. When they all learned that both Eko and Indra were not with the team and the group, they slowly began to leave. Several hours later, the crowds were all gone, and things were just getting started.

After several hours of sleep, the group in Santa Fe were now eating as they always did as a family together. Many questions were asked, and both Eko and Indra wondered when they would be playing baseball. They were excited to start being baseball players. Because of the size of the group and also the outside interest by others for security reasons, it was decided that the first official baseball practice would only have Roger, Eko, and Indra attending from their group in Santa Fe. Idah was going to stay behind with the other villagers in Santa Fe, for she completely trusted Roger to watch the twins and take care of them. As a helicopter arrived at the estate, everyone gathered and wished Eko and Indra a good first baseball practice with the team. It took them nearly thirty minutes to arrive from Santa Fe to the baseball stadium via helicopter, and as the helicopter arrived at the stadium, it was seen entering and landing in the middle of the baseball field for the Conquistadors.

All of the team, the players, the coaches, and everyone on the staff were present to meet and see Eko and Indra arrive. The reporter, Susan Vallelunga, and cameraman, Jeff Ohm, were also present, and they only media allowed. Sheldon then gave Eko and Indra the official tour of the stadium. The two brothers were impressed on how big the stadium is, and Indra told Roger, *"Roger, this is beautiful and sure is unlike anything I ever imagined."*

The brothers decided that this tour was taking too long, so they decide that they would see and do a tour themselves. It took them a matter of moments, and they saw everything inside the stadium, even Ron's research and development room. Both of the twins then asked Roger and Sheldon, *"Can we have some practice? We have seen everything and are ready to play baseball."*

Sheldon looked at the both of them *"Yes, it is time. Let's get to practice. But first,* let us do some batting practice, "as always Eko, being the oldest, was first to bat. Coach DJ, the pitching coach, would be the pitcher, and Coach Mike would catch for Coach DJ.

First up was Eko; Ron, meanwhile, was happy to be able to test out the final changes that he had made for the equipment and see how efficient everything worked. First pitch to Eko and a wrist flick, *"HOME RUN,"*

The second Pitch to Eko,*"HOME RUN!"*

Every pitch to Eko that is hittable was a HOME RUN, regardless of hitting as a left-handed or a right-handed hitter. Indra had the exact same results; HOME RUN after HOME RUN. Sheldon, Ron, Bill, and Roger were very happy to see that the netting was indeed doing as intended. It was stopping, and not having the baseballs being hit turned into something dangerous or deadly. It worked, and that gave Sheldon quite a bit of peace of mind for fan safety.

By this time, Sheldon received a call and was informed that the Commissioner of Baseball was at the stadium and would like to see Eko and Indra himself and what they could do. After all, he had yet to see either of them personally. Sheldon approved, and by the time the Commissioner arrived, Indra was just finishing up his batting practice. Coach Chaves then asked Eko and Indra to get ready for pitching and catching practice. This was the first time that either Eko or Indra had a glove that fit.

Eko took a player's glove, and Indra took the catcher's mitt. As they got into position, Roger asked the commissioner, *"Would you like to bat against them, Mr. Commissioner? That way, you can feel the air being generated by the pitches."* The Commissioner declined, and Coach Chaves decided that he would be the first to stand in the batter's box.

Coach Chaves asked Eko, *"Eko, don't you need any warm-up pitches?"* Eko replied, *"No, Coach Chaves, I am ready, are you ready?"* Coach Chaves nodded that he was ready, and Eko said, *"Ok, Coach, 1, 2, 3"* and then pitched.

Ron and Roger were both monitoring the system for this would be the first time that they were able to record the actual pitching speed; now that the new radar gun now had four digits capable of recording the true pitch speed. Just like on the Island, a perfect unseen pitch that was recorded by the radar gun was at 1,064 miles per hour. Ron then laughed, *"I guess my math on the Island was accurate." Ron thought to himself.*

Roger looked at Ron and agreed. This went on for thirty minutes, and never once did the speed or accuracy drop. Roger yelled out to Eko, *"OK, Eko, and time to use your other arm."*

Eko disappeared from the pitcher's mound, and in less than a second, he was back with the other baseball glove so he could now pitch using his other arm. For the next thirty minutes using the other arm, they received the exact same results; perfect pitches each and every time at 1,064 miles per hour with perfect accuracy. The Commissioner and the teammates were stunned and speechless.

Now, it was Indra's turn, and just like his older twin brother, had the exact same results. Pitch after pitch and never even slowing down or missing the target. Between the two of them, Eko and Indra threw nearly 5,000 pitches in a little over two hours, and all of them had been perfect dead center strikes verified by Ron's technology.

During the entire time, Susan and Jeff had been filming this entire experience, and, as the practice was about to end, they approached Sheldon and the Baseball Commissioner. Susan asked the Commissioner, *"Well, Mr. Commissioner. Now that you have seen this for yourself, what do you think?"*

He responded with, *"I am very thankful for all this safety equipment that we are having installed. Furthermore, I am somewhat in shock that seeing what I have seen is even possible, yet it is."*

Sheldon then whispered into Susan's ear, *"Susan, go and get that video out and available to the other media members."*

Susan nodded her head and gestured to Jeff to follow her as they left the field. Within a matter of moments, the footage was spread all over all forms of media from the internet, television, radio, and even print. As the word spread this was happening, the video was now sought after by now billions of people worldwide.

It was just a few weeks ago that both Eko and Indra were nobody that anyone knew, or had heard of. Yet, as of now, they were undoubtedly the two most recognized people on the entire planet. Thousands of others, after seeing this, also wanted to place future bets on the Conquistadors to win that season's World Series.

However, all the sportsbooks, both legal and illegal, were no longer accepting this bet. Without a doubt, it was the first year, and the first Season of the original longest of long shots to win this year's World Series. Without a game of the regular season, even played were now the biggest favorites to win the World Series.

As the practice was finally over and after the team head to the locker room to shower and change, the word that Eko and Indra were at practice was confirmed by Susan's footage. The crowds outside the ballpark had grown to the largest size, yet, to date, everyone wanted to see these twins for themselves. Those that wanted to have their season tickets refunded were now very happy that they still had them. For the Eko and Indra show to be seen would indeed be the biggest tickets of all time.

Even though some of the other thirty-five teams were upset, one thing was certain, no matter where the Conquistadors were to play, they would ensure that those games would be 100% sold out. This was something that the other five expansion teams were happy with, along with most of the other Professional Teams. Within a matter of minutes, the Conquistadors away games were all sold out to each and every away game as well as all home games.

Chapter 8
The Season

Opening Weekend for the Major League Baseball was starting, and the hottest tickets were anywhere that the Conquistadors would be playing. Opening up in their new built Stadium, the Conquistadors would be playing the Los Angeles Dodgers, which was one of the top teams in the National League. The people had been outside the stadium waiting for this moment. The season ticket holders that sold a ticket for this game alone made more money than the entire season cost. The people all over the world were either in attendance or attempting to purchase a ticket for the hottest event in decades.

The President of the United States was in attendance as Sheldon Winn's guest in the owner's skybox. On each side of the box was Eko and Indra's entire family and tribe, who would have these boxes for the entire season. The two most famous people in the entire World was Eko and Indra, yet most people did not even know much about either one. Sheldon had gone up and beyond in order to ensure that they were well protected and also kept all information about them. Some of the other owners made official complaints in regards to Eko and Indra. One of the owners even requested additional testing to be done to ensure that nothing such as P.E.D., otherwise known as Personal Enhancement Drugs or *"Steroids,"* or anything of that nature was done for either Eko or Indra. Yet, of course, all of the tests came back negative, and everything about the twins was indeed natural and not scientific.

Even all the big four television stations made an agreement that the day's opening game would be televised on FOX, NBC, CBS, and ABC along with over a hundred countries worldwide. As the gates finally opened, it took minutes for all the team shops to be completely sold out. Not only did all the Conquistador team merchandise sell out at the Stadium, but it was sold out everywhere else. Eko and Indra, prior to even playing a single game, had increased the entire league's merchandised and ticket sales by nearly a hundred billion dollars.

They also had generated enough interest worldwide that baseball overtook Football, or as the American's would say, *"Soccer,"* as the worlds most watched and followed sport, even in the areas that didn't have baseball. No one, not even Roger or Sheldon, thought that it would be like it is. Even the Commissioner and the majority of the other

Owners were happy with the new bottom line for Major League Baseball. The announcer was now announcing the visiting team, the Los Angeles Dodgers, and they would be batting first since they were the visiting team. Then they announced the starting line-up for the Albuquerque Conquistadors: *"Batting first and Pitching will be Eko Suparman, Batting second and Catching will be Indra Suparman."* The crowd noise is so loud that no one could even hear the rest of the starting lineup.

Not just is the stadium at full packed capacity on the outside, hundreds of thousands of fans from all over the World were also there at the stadium. Sheldon knew that the tickets would indeed sellout for each and every home game, and so, as a gesture for goodwill towards all these fans had on the outside of the stadium put up several large monitors for those fans to view and also watch.

By adding their presence to the area, the crowd noise was twenty times greater than that of any sporting event ever. As like every time before, Eko didn't even warm-up or have a desire to warm up as the game is about to start. Since the umpire and field officials were no longer part of the officiating, Ron's tech was now at every baseball stadium and being used by the Conquistadors yet at each and every stadium having games. Even some of the other owners were broadcasting that day's game to their fans at their home stadiums, which had never happened before. It was as one of the owners put it, *"We are only doing this to ensure our own fans show up, and if we need to broadcast the Conquistadors games to get fans into our seats, we shall do that."*

And they did exactly that for many baseball fans. Even if they had another team, they cheered because they still wanted to be part of the day's historical event: "*Eko and Indra's first game ever.*"

The game was officially started, and on the Mound facing the Dodgers leadoff hitter was Eko. The computer mentioned that it was game time, and Eko stood in front of nearly 70,000 fans inside and another 300,000 or more fans outside and threw his first pitch.

The crowd couldn't even follow or see the pitch for the baseball was traveling at speeds that averaged to 1,064 miles per hour. Just as Eko did on the Island, in practice, he threw a perfect pitch. *"Strike One"* was shown on the system. The next eight pitches were all strikes. The top of the first inning was over with only nine pitches thrown, and not a single batter made any contact with the pitches for they were pitched and delivered faster than any Major League hitter could even swing a baseball bat. With three up and three down in the top of the first, the Conquistadors were now up to bat. First up was Eko facing last year's National League Cy Young Winner, the best pitcher in the National League. As the Dodgers pitcher delivered the first pitch, and with a single arm; with just a flick of his wrist, Eko crushed the ball so hard that it hits the adamantium vibriam protective net and crushed. It was Home Run, and even better, the netting indeed did protect the fans in the area as well.

The Score was now 0-1 in favor of the Conquistadors, and before Indra could come up to bat, the Pitching Coach for the Dodgers called a time out. As the pitching coach was at the mound, the catcher and the rest of the infielders joined the Coach at the Mound. Coach told them to intentionally *"Walk"* Indra, especially after a home run on the very first pitch. He told them all, *"Hey, let's just give the next hitter a pass and then work on getting the next three batters out and leave this first inning just down a run."* They all agreed, especially the pitcher. So Indra then entered the batter box batting left-handed. The catcher then moved out of his position to his far left side, way outside the strike zone. After four pitches, Indra was given an intentional walk to first base. As soon as the computer stated ball four, and a walk signal appeared, Indra laid down the baseball bat and then, at the same time, as the Catcher was throwing back the baseball to the Pitcher, Indra took off and before the Pitcher could even catch the throw back, Indra had touched all the bases and the home plate, making the score zero for the Dodgers and two Runs for the Conquistadors.

Immediately, the Head Manager of the Dodgers was out and throwing a protest. However, without any officials on the field, he was forced to go back to the Dodgers bench and make a phone call to challenge that last play. As the cameras were following this official protest, it was shown on the screen as a legal and also good run scored.

The protest was not upheld because Indra did indeed touch all the other bases and home plate legally and not tagged out. The fans and the world were stunned because no one ever had seen a play like that before. Each and every batter from the Dodgers were struck out with only three pitches. Every time that Eko or Indra were batting, they either hit a home run or were intentionally walked.

The only times that they were not able to score would be when another Conquistador teammate was on the base in front of them. If no one was on base at the time of the intentional walk, then they always made it home prior to the catcher throwing the pitch back to the pitcher. As the first game came to an end, the official statistics were eighty-one pitches thrown by Eko, twenty-seven batters faced, and not a single ball pitched was called a ball or any runners even advance to first base.

The first-ever perfect game was played and pitched in the entire history of baseball with the Conquistadors winning 12-0 and did that in only eight innings of batting. Since they were the home team, they didn't even bat in the bottom of the ninth inning. After the game, nearly all the fans were still at the ballpark cheering for Eko and Indra.

Not only did they not want to leave, for they had been the first to witness a perfect game, but they also defeated the team everyone picked to win the National League Division and be in the World Series. After today's game and the world seeing what Eko and Indra were about, the Conquistadors had been instantly named, not only the favorite to win the National League but also to win the World Series. Nearly all the Sportsbooks, both legal and illegal, were no longer accepting bets on the Conquistadors. Being the first of the three games against the Dodgers in the opening weekend by the end of the third game, Eko was 2-0, and Indra, who pitched game 2, was 1-0. They both faced a minimum of twenty-seven batters, and both also pitched only eighty-one pitches each. Not a single ball was called one time during the opening 3-game stand, and only the minimum pitches pitched were required of eighty-one pitches per game.

After this 3-game sweep of the Team, many who had previously been picked to be the winner of the National League were now no longer the favorites to win the National League, it was now the Conquistadors who, just a few months ago, were picked to finish dead last and be the worse team in the entire league were now the clear favorites to be the World Series Champions.

After each game, the crowds grew in size, and the Conquistadors were being hit with requests for tickets by the media and the richest people in the world. Sheldon was informed that the media requests worldwide were ten times greater than the number of seats in the stadium. Nothing like this had ever happened in modern times, and Sheldon was very happy because now his team was undoubtedly the most valuable professional team of all sports worldwide. Representatives for just about any item were even greater to have Eko, Indra, or both of the twins. They were never-ending offering nearly fifty billion from a wide variety of possible businesses such as Nike, Under Armor, Adidas, Puma, Coke, Pepsi, Microsoft, PlayStation, Video Game creators, McDonalds, Pizza Hut, Domino's, Taco Bell, Chick Fil A, Burger King, Chevrolet, Ford, Nissan, Toyota, Clothing Manufacturers, and personal hygiene businesses.

Everything which could be sold was seeking Eko and Indra to be representatives and seeking to help with the sales. As the fall classic, better known as the Major League World Series baseball games, where the best teams were the winners of their division to represent the American, and the National League, was approaching. The Conquistadors led by Eko and Indra were still perfect.

They had yet to lose a game, and, more remarkably, they still were perfect, requiring only eighty-one pitches per game. There was still not a single pitch called a ball, and for hitting, Eko and Indra were both still batting a perfect 1,000% batters average. Both of these feats had never happened in the entire recorded history of baseball, and the season was reaching the final point with the playoffs for the World Series Games quickly approaching. Roger suggested to Sheldon that it would be a good time for a break instead of Eko and Indra preparing for the World Series Games. After all, Eko and Indra had been playing baseball and had very little time for any breaks from the game. After Sheldon spoke with Idah to gain her insight about the *"Break,"* Sheldon agreed.

Most of the other teams were not happy that Eko and Indra were going to play in the World Series Games as the National League representative. By now, everyone believed that it would be the Albuquerque Conquistadors winning the World Series in their first season. Sheldon agreed to give Eko and Indra a break, especially since Idah thought it would be the best thing for Eko and Indra. Sheldon asked Idah, *"Idah, what and where would you and twins like to go and relax before the start of the World Series?"*

Idah looked at Sheldon, and with her calm voice, said, *"I want Roger and the rest of our tribe to go back to our Island for a few days, Sheldon. Home will give us a break we need from all the media, where we have always been able to be ourselves."*

Sheldon thought it would be a great idea and agreed to have things set up for the entire group to go back to their Island that had always been home. Many of the fans had purchased tickets for the World Series Game 1, after all, the tickets were sold for nearly 100-1,000 times greater than their face value.

After all, the majority of the players and even some of the players on the Conquistadors were getting tired of all the news always being about Eko and Indra. Some of the other owners of the different baseball teams had been growing with concerns and complaints.

It was not unusual to have owners or players from other teams complain that Eko and Indra were hurting the game or being able not even to compete. After all, not one opposing hitter has even made contact with a single pitch, no balls had been pitched, and it was impossible to strike out either Eko or Indra.

They were truly impossible to compete against even though Eko and Indra had only recently begun to play baseball. And winning the National League in a sweep to continue with the Perfect record, which after the end of the regular season, was going into 162 wins and 0 losses.

Then, to win the first four games in the first round, making their regular season and postseason now at 166 wins and no losses. They met the Chicago Cubs in the National League Championship, and as Eko and Indra had done all season, they went 4-0 and were again perfect. At this time, they were waiting for the two teams in the American League, The Boston Red Sox, and the New York Yankee's to finish their American League Championship. They were tied in the Series 2-2 and would be ten days away from the World Series against the Albuquerque Conquistadors.

Chapter 9
The World Series

With the World Series now waiting for the American League to have a champion between the Red Sox and Yankee's, game 1 of the World Series was ten days away. This was the longest period that Eko or Indra did not have to play a baseball game. However, for Eko and Indra, things never slowed down as many different groups of various advertising agencies were always attempting to have them represent their products.

Different owners from different sports were looking to sign either Eko or Indra as players for different sports such as American Football, World Wide Football, Basketball, Tennis, Bowling, Cricket, Tennis, Mixed Martial *"UFC"* and any other sporting or team sports either in the U.S. or some other country.

For Eko and Indra, any sport was easy, and it was only a matter of hours or days to master it. They did enjoy playing with children, and often, these were the only times they would lose. They loved football, basketball, and flag football when they played with those children. Roger,

Idah, and even Sheldon would often visit them at their home near Santa Fe and were amazed at what they could do in any sporting game. What impressed them, even more, was how humble and down to Earth, both Eko and Indra were. They never made any of the children upset, and they always made sure everyone was included, especially those who wished to play or participate, even if it was hide and seek, tag, or something that children all over the world play.

However, the news eventually leaked out about the compound in Santa Fe, and that created quite a bit of concern for Sheldon. After all, he was very well aware that *"if"* the Conquistadors did win the World Series, the Casinos and other Sportbooks could lose hundreds of billions of dollars. This was a huge concern for somebody who knew what businessmen around the globe would do to protect that type of money.

Sheldon only shared this concern with Roger and Barbara. Roger thought to himself that he was the creator of this since he had placed the biggest bet. This was the bet where if the Conquistadors did win the World Series, it would be 48 billion alone on his winning ticket. Not to mention how many others made bets on the Conquistadors when their odds were 15,000-1 or greater to win the World Series, which they were now four games away from achieving. Knowing this, Roger, Sheldon, and Barbara went to Idah and asked her if she and the others would like to go to St. Thomas rather than back to the island for a few days to get away and have a break. It was an estate that Sheldon owned, which had enough security with few people living on the island. This made it a very safe and secure place for Eko, Indra, and everyone else.

Idah agreed after Sheldon, Roger and Barbara convinced her. Then she informed the rest of the tribe that they were going on a trip for a few days to St. Thomas. This was good, especially as they were seeing how many people were beginning to show up at home in Santa Fe, and the numbers were growing by the minute. Sheldon had Barbara made arrangements for three helicopters to pick everyone up from Santa Fe and then be transported to Kirkland Air Force base for the trip to St. Thomas.

Eko and Indra were excited for they had always loved to travel and visit new places, see new things and experiences. However, they were unaware that this was mainly being done to ensure they would be safe until the start and finish of the upcoming World Series, which was nine days away. As they arrived in St. Thomas, they were thrilled. The weather was considerably warmer and to be near the sea again was something that all the villagers had indeed missed. To hear the ocean and to see the stars at night reminded them of the lives they had lived before they moved to New Mexico. Sheldon had hired triple the normal security to ensure things would be safe and made sure that they could all relax before the biggest event for all of them was about to begin *"The World Series."* They could see that the finish was now within reach and that all they had hoped and dreamed of was coming to fruition and hopefully turning into reality.

With less than five days before Game 1 of the World Series, it was finally determined that the New York Yankee's would be the Team to meet the upstart Albuquerque Conquistadors. *"Who is better?"* Sheldon thought. After all, the New York Yankee's had more appearances and championships than any other baseball team. It was being billed as the battle of the old guard versus the new. Some called it David versus Goliath, yet this time, the Conquistadors were not David; rather, they were the Goliaths, even being a first-year team. They were going 170-0 in the regular season and the postseason, as well as being the first-ever team to have a completely perfect season *"ever."* However, they were still 4 games away from being the World Series Champions. During the time at St. Thomas, Idah had noticed how Eko and Indra had become rather close to both Aspyn Walling and Susan Vallelunga. Eko and Indra, for the very first time in their lives, were wanting to spend time with these two women. Eko asked Idah if he and Susan could spend time alone together.

Shortly after that, Indra asked Idah if he and Aspyn could spend time alone as well. Naturally, Idah agreed and let Sheldon and Roger know that she gave them permission to go and spend some time alone.

Sheldon wasn't too thrilled about this and told both Idah and Roger, *"Well, they couldn't have picked a worse time. I really think they should wait until the end of the World Series and then go and do anything they wish to do."*

Roger looked at Idah and saw that she wasn't too happy with Sheldon on what he stated. He then looked at Sheldon and said, *"Well Sheldon, as their agent and also a person that cares very much for Eko and Indra, I disagree.*

However, I think that you should tell Idah about your concern. The concern that you and Barbara told me and why we came to St. Thomas in the first place."

Idah had her eyes frozen on Sheldon and asked him right away, *"What does Roger know, and what have you not been telling me?"*

Being concerned, Sheldon dropped his head and replied, *"Idah, I didn't want you or anyone to worry, but there are a lot of people that do not want to see Eko and Indra lead our team to the World Series Championship. Some of those people are very bad, and well, they could do harm or something even worse to Eko, Indra, or both of them."*

Idah continued, *"Why would someone or anyone wish to hurt Eko or Indra?"*

Sheldon answered, *"I can give you sixty-eight billion reasons, Idah."*

Idah was still unable to understand and stared at Sheldon with a confused look. Roger then explained to Idah how he had placed a bet for them to win the World Series and that if the Conquistadors did win, then he would earn $48 billion and the other $20 billion or more would go to others who also placed a bet on the Conquistadors to win the World Series. He also explained how some Casinos and Sport's books were controlled by the MOB, and that the MOB may do things to protect that money instead of losing it, even kill. Idah was terrified for that was something she never imagined; however, she knew and also agreed that this wasn't the time for them to go anywhere away from the estate or to leave the grounds. Never had Idah had such fears.

The last time she did was when she was a young woman, and it eventually led to her fleeing and going to the island that they had called home for many years, till they left for New Mexico. She wasn't happy, yet she trusted Roger and now knew that Sheldon, too, was concerned for not just Eko and Indra, but all of them, including Idah and the others from the tribe.

When she informed both Eko and Indra that they could spend time alone with Susan and Aspyn, they would have to do so at the estate and would not be allowed to leave the grounds. Eko and Indra were not happy, and this was the first time that Idah had made a decision, and then she changed her mind. They were only twenty years old and wondered, as well as asked if they had done something not to allow them to go and see the sites in St. Thomas. Idah was speechless and didn't even give them an answer; after all, she was still somewhat in a shock and had no words to share with them; neither did she want to scare them. Naturally, they both were extremely upset, and even Roger and Sheldon had never seen either Eko or Indra upset before. They knew that this would be best, and so Sheldon asked Roger to speak to both of them in an attempt to smooth things over. Roger agreed and immediately went to Eko and Indra to discuss and try to reason with them without telling them the entire reason why.

Roger sat down while Eko and Indra were standing right in front of him and began talking, *"Eko, Indra, you know, that I love both of you like my own children. I, Idah, and everyone else do care very, very much for you two. I will make you a deal right here and right now. We are all leaving tomorrow to head back to Albuquerque, and instead of going straight back to Santa Fe, how about you two along with Susan, Aspyn, Idah, myself, and a few others take some time together before game 1 of the World Series? After the World Series, we can go anywhere and do anything you both would like."*

Indra interrupted and asked, *"Roger, after the World Series, can we go back home to our Island? Not forever, but just for a while; we miss the ocean and the stars."*

Roger spontaneously agreed, *"Yes, we can, and if you like, we can bring Aspyn and Susan too. I think they would like to spend time with you and Eko."*

Both the twins smiled and calmed down. They knew that they could do what they wished as soon as the season was over. It was all they needed to know. It was now game one of the World Series, and since the Conquistadors had the best all-time record of having a hundred percent winning percentage, they got home-field advantage.

Tickets were impossible to get unless one was willing to pay several hundred thousand for standing room, and the premiere seats were selling in millions. It was a 'who is who' in attendance. Movie Stars, billionaires, and high-end millionaires, along with the world's most powerful people, were present there.

Even the President of the United States and the President of the Republic of Indonesia were guests at Sheldon's own booth. Being the World Series meant that it was quite a bit more than the playoff games, due to which the crowd outside the ballpark was estimated in millions. Albuquerque was not prepared or able to handle the crowd if anything were to go wrong during this.

The announcers called out the starting lineup and started off with the Yankee's as they are the visiting team and were to bat first. Everyone was waiting to see what Sheldon would do for the Conquistadors announcement. It was Sheldon himself that announced the Conquistadors starting lineup while getting ready to announce the music playing: the one from the Superman movie.

It was how the Conquistadors announced their starting lineup. *"Batting first and pitching; you know him, you love him. He's undefeated and oldest of the two, Eko, the firstborn! And batting second and catching tonight is Indra the 'Strong One.'"*

It continued until all the remaining nine starters were announced. The first inning was about to begin as Eko and Indra had done all season, they appeared almost as if by magic instantly in their respective positions. Eko didn't even take any warm-up pitches just like he had done all season long. The automatic system indicated that it was time to play ball. The first nine pitches were invisible to everyone, as usual. However, by the system, they were all perfect strikes. Three Yankees Up and Three Yankees were out, and the first inning was over.

By the end of the first inning, Eko was up to bat. As usual, he only used one hand to hold the bat as if it were a pencil. The Pitcher looked at the catcher, and after getting the signal for the pitch, it instantly hit Eko. It would have hurt anyone, yet the ball hitting Eko was like a fly landing on one's hand. No pain, it was just annoyance.

The system indicated that the pitcher hit the batter, "Eko," so he was instantly awarded a free pass to first base. Eko laid down the bat gently, and before the catcher could throw the ball back to the pitcher, Eko stole 2nd, 3rd, and home. All of this was before the baseball was even retrieved by the Pitcher. The score then was Yankee's 0 and Conquistadors' 1.

The manager of the Yankees called a timeout and then proceeded to the pitcher's mound, where he met the pitcher and the catcher, while the other infielders had also arrived at the mound. They discussed a few things before everyone went back to their positions as the coach was leaving back toward the dugout. As Indra entered the box to bat 2nd, the catcher jumped out from his catcher's position, for they were going to give Indra an intentional walk.

After four balls, the system indicated that Indra had been awarded an intentional walk and had free passage to first base. Like Eko, Indra gently placed the bat down, and as the catcher was throwing the baseball back to the pitcher, Indra crossed the second and third base and touched the home plate prior to the baseball's arrival to the pitcher.

It was now 2-0 in favor of the Conquistadors and no outs. Game One of the World Series ended up being 6-0 with the Conquistadors winning game one. Eko and Indra scored every time they were up and did not even register a hit. They were intentionally walked and were not even pitched. Only eighty-one pitches were required by Eko to win.

Game two was Indra's turn to pitch and Eko to catch, yet the batting order remained the same. Eko, being the firstborn and oldest, had always gone first. Some would ask if Indra was jealous or upset about that; however, that never bothered him and was never an issue for Indra.

Indra won game two with a score of 7-0, and like his brother the day earlier, it was eighty-one perfect pitches, and both were either walked or struck by the pitch. Neither had a chance to even swing at any of the pitches.

With it now being 2-0 in the best of seven games, all the Conquistadors needed was two more wins and could close out the season at Yankee Stadium. This was the first time that Eko and Indra would be at the Yankee Stadium. Yes, they played the New York Mets in New York, but this was Yankee Stadium, the team with a phenomenal history in all of Major League Baseball.

Sheldon and Roger were concerned that if anything were to happen badly or intentionally, it would happen here in New York. They all knew that, without Eko and Indra playing, the Conquistadors would be run over by the Yankees. With billions at stake, they knew that if something were to happen, then this would be the time and place. After all, even billions could not replace Eko or Indra.

In a huge city like New York, many would think that it would be easy to keep a secret, especially with millions of residents and tons of tourists at any given time. The tourism was far greater than it had ever been, for it was like everyone in the world wanted to be in New York for the World Series. History was about to be made, not by just winning the World Series, but by being completely perfect without even a single loss or even a run being scored against the Conquistadors all season.

Sheldon had attempted to keep the team's location a top-secret, but the employees that worked at the hotel had leaked it with the media. There was one thing that no one thought of or considered was to attack the entire team, which included both Eko and Indra. Most of them figured that someone who had ties to the Casino and Sportsbook would commit such an act of attacking a team.

When the Conquistadors arrived at their hotel and had their supper, everyone who ate and drank the food and beverages became rather ill. Even for Eko and Indra, it was hard to determine if it was poisoning or some substance to make them all sick. It was so bad that several of the teammates, wives, girlfriends, children, even Susan and Aspyn became ill.

They were required to go to the hospital and seek medical attention. With game three soon to take place, it would be a miracle if the Conquistadors could even field a team of nine required players. Eko and Indra recovered far quicker than most, yet everyone else, especially the youngsters, along with the women, were far sicker and couldn't even leave the hospital. The game was now just a few hours away; Sheldon and Coach Chaves were trying to see if they could get seven more fostered players able to suit up for the game.

Chapter 10
Homecoming

The sooner that Eko and Indra wanted to get home, the more they were made to wait. They were desperately counting the days and wanting the season to get over to spend some valuable time with Susan and Aspyn. The attack on their health had delayed their visit to Indonesia, and all they could do was wait patiently. Once the news of this became public, quite a bit of rioting had started to happen in New York and nearby areas.

The baseball commissioner decided that, after learning of this, game three was to be postponed due to the recent events for the integrity of the game. It was more important for the team, and everyone affected to recover.

With game three now canceled until further notice, an investigation was pending regarding the poisoning of the Conquistadors.Eko and Indra had indeed recovered quicker than any of the others. The doctors said that it was because of how they burned off calories; it certainly helped them in recovering faster.

Eko and Indra were worried about those that were part of the family *"Conquistadors "*and also those in their tribe that had the same meal and were affected. As Eko and Indra were taking an elevator to another level, they were accompanied by a short well-dressed man who appeared to be in his mid-forties. Once the elevator closed, the man with only Eko and Indra present said, *"Eko, Indra, if you really care and do not want anything bad to happen, then you will lose the next four games and let the Yankee's win the World Series."*

Both Eko and Indra were confused, and since they had good nature, excellent character, and were down to earth, they didn't realize that this man just threatened them. As the door of the elevator opened, the man left, and both Eko and Indra looked at each other and shrugged it off. They then continued to go further up in the elevator to the other level. The hospital was crowded with their family, friends, and teammates. They went to see Idah first, who was sharing a room with Roger.

Indra told Idah and Roger what happened, and instantly, Roger grabbed the phone in the hospital room and asked for security. As security entered the hospital room, Roger narrated the events that just happened. The security officer immediately called for a lockdown of the hospital and contacted the New York Police Department. Sheldon and Barbara in the room next door heard the commotion, and as people were running by, they opened the door to enter the hospital room.

Sheldon flagged down a staff member who told Sheldon what had happened. Sheldon was still extremely weak and unable to get out of bed due to the poisoning. He grabbed his cell phone and called the President of the United States. Thirty minutes later, the hospital was filled with FBI, Home Land Security, CIA, and other members of federal and local law enforcement.

As they reviewed the footage of the elevator and other areas in and out of the hospital, not one image showed a picture of the man's face who threatened the Suparman brothers. The Commissioner was now aware of this, and so was the owner of the Yankee's baseball team. Rumors were being leaked out of the hospital, and more and more people had gathered outside. Some of the rumors were that Eko and Indra had been killed.

Later that evening, it was announced by the Commissioner that games three and four were postponed and were rescheduled to be played a week later under heavy security before, during, and after the games. Any attack was not acceptable.

One week later, without any more issues, everyone was back to being normal and feeling better. Game three was also back on. Again, Eko had pitched a perfect game and was now leading the series 3-0 and needing only one more win to be the World Series Champions.

For game four, the security was doubled, and martial law was put into effect in a five-mile area surrounding the Yankee's Baseball Stadium. This was done by the Mayor requesting the Governor, and then the Governor asking the President to enforce what they had all agreed upon.

Game four began as expected and planned with Indra pitching. Indra pitched the perfect eighty-one pitches, and for the first time in the history of Major League Professional Baseball, it was indeed a perfect season. This was perfect both in terms of wins, and also that no runs were scored against the Conquistadors. Eko and Indra both had a perfect batting average, which made the

Conquistadors the World Series Champions. Roger had won $48 billion, and Sheldon's team now was worth nearly a trillion dollars, exceeding any other team in any sport in terms of net worth. After game four of the World Series Championship, Roger and Idah congratulated Eko and Indra as well as everyone in the Conquistadors organization.

Sheldon, Barbara, Susan, and Aspyn, along with the other teammates, joined them. Eko looked at Roger and reminded him, *"You know what you promised us, Roger. Now that the season is done, we can go to our island for homecoming, and Indra and I want to bring Susan and Aspyn with us."*

Roger agreed, and so did everyone else, for it was long overdue. Eko and Indra won every award together. They were named co-winners of the MVP, as well as the co-winners of the National League CY Young. The team had a perfect 174 wins and not a single loss. They allowed zero runs to be scored against them, and both Eko and Indra batted to perfection. It was, without a doubt, the *"Perfect Season."*

History was made, and it was made by the team which everyone had picked to finish with the worse record prior to the signing of Eko and Indra. During Baseball's conclusion of the World Series and after the World Series Parade with Eko and Indra leading the way to the World Championship, they were excited to go to a homecoming. Nearly nine months had passed since Roger took them all from the island to go and play baseball for the Conquistadors.

The media alone was chasing them 24/7; they were attempting non-stop meets and still wanted more information on Eko and Indra. As for the biggest corporations in the world; Apple, Amazon.com, Alphabet, Microsoft, Facebook, Alibaba, were just a few of the biggest corporations that were constantly seeking a way to have Eko and Indra as brand ambassadors for their businesses.

Along with that, a large number of owners for other professional sports such as football, American Football *"NFL"*, Basketball *"NBA"*, Tennis, Boxing, UFC, and other sporting events teams also wanted the opportunity to have both Eko and Indra, or at least one of them to sign to their team as well.

Aside from the fans, the media and companies all wanted some time with Eko and Indra. The homecoming was indeed something that everyone like Eko, Indra, Idah, Roger, and the other people of the tribe were looking forward to. Sheldon was with the group as they were landing in Jakarta, and with the help of the Government of the Republic of Indonesia, he made sure that it was safe and that they were able to land without the fans or media knowing about it. It was somewhat very secretive as only Sheldon, the passengers, and the President of Indonesia were aware of their short visit.

As they landed at a private airfield in Jakarta, they all were greeted by the President of Indonesia and his staff. This was the first time that the Indonesian President had an opportunity to meet Eko, Indra, and Idah personally in real life. Like everyone else, the President also wished to meet them and wanted something from Eko and Indra.

However, this first meeting was not the time nor the place for the President to make requests. As soon as they arrived, they were immediately transferred to two helicopters to make the journey back to the island. On the way toward their island, they noticed that, since their last departure, many things had changed, all because of the Suparman brothers. Many of the corporations and even different sporting leagues, in a short period of time, had all created local businesses and bases of operations. Many thought that perhaps there were others similar to Eko and Indra, and the only way was to have local long-term staff in place.

Along with having a presence in Indonesia, some of these corporations thought that it might be a way to have an in and get one or both of them signed as representatives or brand ambassadors of their products. Not to mention that the overall purchasing power for all residents of Indonesia had greatly increased because of the twins. Life in Indonesia had never been more prosperous than at this time for the residents, and it was because of what they called the *"Eko and Indra Effect."*

Tourism had increased 100,000 times more, adding greatly to their economy. Indonesia had never had such a stable economy for decades, and the people were thankful to Conquistadors. Thousands of islands that were once not inhabited were now blooming with factories, manufacturing plants, and businesses. None of which would have happened without the 'Eko and Indra Effect.'

When they saw what had happened to their home, they were all shocked, and some were even upset that it was a different place. Nike had taken over what was recently home to the tribe. Idah was very upset because the island was now a place of industry and business. As they landed on the island, they were greeted by Dolores Thomas, who was the regional in-charge of the new Nike Manufacturing Plant and offices set up in Indonesia.

Dolores was not expecting that the arriving members from the Village were going to be upset. It was heartbreaking to see what was once a very beautiful island now had transformed into a place of business filled with many people. Dolores was at a loss for words and had no idea that this would be the result or cause of creating an upsetting feeling for Eko, Indra, and the other villagers. Their home was now gone and would never be the same.

The President of Indonesia informed Idah and the others that this was a very good thing for the country as well as the residents. After all, Indonesia was now a powerhouse in terms of economy and growth. Never had the entire country been better off. However, he, like Dolores, did not even think that this would be an issue, even though it did bother all the villagers.

Some of the village members were, prior to this event, even thinking of staying at *"Home."* Yet, the sight of this instantly changed their minds. This was no longer *"home,"* as they knew it, and they also realized those days of what it was, were no longer going to be the same. After all, this was supposed to be a homecoming, and also a time for all of them to have some peace and spend some quality time in a familiar environment.

They wanted to have some privacy at *"home,"* but that wasn't going to happen now. The Indonesian President asked Idah if she and the rest of them would like to go back to the capital city and stay at his place for the night. He gave them the chance to eat, rest, and be his guests at the President's residency. Having limited options, they all agreed and were on the way from the island back to the mainland. This was the time when the Indonesian President decided would be the best time to present his request.

As he was sitting near Idah, Eko, and Indra, he looked up to all of them and stated, *"We, as in myself and all the residents are so very proud of what you three have done for our country. And this request is not just from me; rather, it is from all of us; every citizen wants to see you play. While you are here, we hope to have Eko and Indra be able to perform against an All-Star Asia Baseball Team, a World Wide Football and World Wide Basketball game events in Indonesia. It will be for the people of Indonesia, which we will broadcast to the entire world to see. We also hope that both Eko and Indra will be the two that will participate as Indonesians for both the winter and summer Olympics as well. This is something that will bring Indonesia pride, and we would be able to compete against any and all the other countries in the entire world. We request Eko and Indra to lead."*

Upon hearing this, Sheldon replied, *"That would take some time for the three events that you wish, Mr. President, to have the baseball, football, and basketball organized, and it would be up to Eko and Indra to make that decision."*

The President replied, *"No, Mr. Winn. That will not be a problem for all three of these events that could take place in a week or two, possibly, or even less than two weeks."*

Idah then went on to ask, *"How is that possible? That decision will be up to Eko and Indra if they wish to do that."*

At that time, both Eko and Indra agreed that they would certainly love to participate in the local community, especially since it would be in Indonesia. They knew that it would allow the local people a chance to see them compete, not just in baseball, but in other sports as well.

Even though Sheldon was reluctant, he knew that it would keep Eko and Indra happy, and they agreed to it. As for the Olympics, they were not to happen for another year till the Summer and then three more years for the Winter Olympics. However, Eko and Indra agreed to be the members of both the winter and summer games representing Indonesia.

As they arrived at the President's home, they all finally had the opportunity to get some rest. After all, they would need it, especially since they were to have the three sporting events very soon at the remodeled Taman Duta Mas Sports Center.

Chapter 11
The Asian Baseball All-Stars game

They arrived for the first event at the Taman Duta Mas Sports Center, which was remodeled because of the money they had earned in that blissful economy. Baseball was to be played first. The Indonesian team consisted of Eko, Indra, and the rest of the villagers from the tribe to compete against the current greatest baseball players of the time. The entire event was free for the locals, and hundreds of thousands of them had come to attend.

Many members of the media were also present from various networks worldwide. However, the only network allowed to broadcast was the state-run station, TVRI, for the local broadcast. Meanwhile, Susan and Jeff had permission to cover the tournament on a global level. Even though everyone in Indonesia had seen Eko and Indra on television, this was the first time they had a chance to see them in person. The crowd was very excited to see them play baseball live.

Like every other sport, they had the Indonesian national anthem played first and then followed by the Asian anthems of countries that had a representative of their country in the All-Star players team. During the introduction, the home team was called the *"Emerald of the Equator."* While the names of the players were announced, the theme song of *"Superman"* played, which was similar to how Sheldon did in games of the Conquistador Season.

They had the exact same results which they had during the season in which Eko faced twenty-seven batters, needing the same eighty-one pitches, and both Eko and Indra batted excellently as usual. It was a perfect game, just like every other game they had played before. They were the World Series Champions of Major League Baseball, and now they were also Champions of various Asian Baseball Leagues such as the *"Emerald of the Equator."*

The team representing Indonesia had won the game 8-0, and it was against the very best Asian Baseball players. By this time, everyone who played baseball in any professional leagues, regardless of the country, were all using the exact same system, which was used in Major

League Baseball. The Pay Per View exceeded 2 billion purchases and was a major success ensuring that the Indonesian government would be able to take care of all the citizens for a very long time. As the game ended, the crowd in the stadium ran across the baseball field to congratulate the team, especially Eko and Indra, for their victory. They were mostly locals, and they were very proud of how Eko and Indra had represented their country across the world. Eko and Indra had, at this point, proven to the entire world that they were both the greatest athletes of all time.

"We have the greatest athletes of all time," the President of Indonesia announced in the closing ceremony held right after the game. The President was very pleased, and Eko and Indra had exceeded even his greatest hopes.

The crowd was silently listening to their President's address when a local interrupted and screamed from the crowd. *"No! They are not the greatest of all time; rather, they are two of the three."* The entire crowd stared at the man who started this. Roger Schafer instantly knew who it was when he saw the man speaking. It was none other than Mahadiyi Suparman, the pilot that Roger Schafer thought had died while flying Roger. He was the one who led to the discovery of Eko and Indra. Roger instantly ran toward Mahadiyi, because after all, if it wasn't for him, Roger wouldn't have survived.

Roger lit up, seeing him, and was extremely happy that he survived. Susan and Jeff followed Roger while simultaneously recording. Roger sprinted toward him, saying, *"This is the man that saved me. He is the reason I was able to meet both Eko and Indra."*

Roger was very excited to see Mahadiyi alive. Although Mahadiyi couldn't have known himself, despite it, none of this would have ever happened without him. The Conquistadors would not have won the World Series. Roger introduced Mahadiyi to everyone and noticed something which he hadn't realized earlier; the pilot looked a lot like Eko and Indra.

Since they had the same last names, Roger wondered if they had any relation to each other. Suparman is a common last name in Indonesia, but at that moment, Roger never thought twice. He had a strong doubt that the three of them were somehow related. Roger asked Mahadiyi to join him, and Mahadiyi agreed happily. As both of them were making their way through the crowd, which was still celebrating the victory, Roger asked Mahadiyi if he knew Eko and Indra. Mahadiyi replied with a grin, *"Yes, I do, Roger. Doesn't everyone know them?"*

Roger then rephrased to ask more precisely as his curiosity was rising, *"Mahadiyi, what I want to ask, or rather, what I mean to ask you is if you had known them before they were famous?"* Mahadiyi turned toward Roger, smiled, and replied, *"Yes, they are my long lost twin nephews who all thought were lost to the Sea."* Roger instantly stopped walking, grabbed Mahadiyi to gain his attention, and asked Mahadiyi if the accident was on purpose. He stared in the pilot's eyes, and that look was not a happy one. Mahadiyi clarified that it was an accident, and his plane was completely destroyed.

He tried repairing it after recovering as he too was injured a great deal. However, the plane was so damaged that it couldn't be repaired. At this time, Eko and Indra had made their way to Roger and Mahadiyi. They were unaware that this man with Roger was a member of their family. This was the first time they had met a relative of theirs. Roger introduced them all to each other, and by this time, Idah, Sheldon, Aspyn, Susan, and the President of Indonesia were all with them. The President recalled that

Mahadiyi was the man who shouted out while he was addressing the crowd.

Both the President and Mahadiyi exchanged greetings and introductions, and so did everyone else. Roger then informed everyone that he was the Pilot who saved him, and also led to the discovery of Eko and Indra on their Island. The Indonesian President was still looking at him, thinking about what he said to him intruding his speech. He asked Mahadiyi what he meant, as his statement had raised quite a few questions in his mind.

This time, the President asked Mahadiyi with the microphone so everyone could hear his answer. The proceedings were covered live, and millions of people around the world awaited Mahadiyi's response. The President asked Mahadiyi, who was then on the big screen, *"What do you mean two of three? Do you mean that there is a third one like Eko and Indra?"* Mahadiyi resolved the mystery and answered, *"Akashi Shiganosuke, he is related to both Eko and Indra."* Roger, Sheldon, and the President were stunned, and at the same time, asked where Akashi Shiganosuke was.

Mahadiyi told them that he had died. He was a Sumo wrestler who lived from 1600-1649. He was eight feet and six inches tall and was a wrestler from 1624-1643. He, too, was the greatest of his time. Akashi was related to Eko and Indra's Mother, who died many years ago while giving birth to her twin boys. He also said that Akashi was very quick and had great speed, just like the Suparman brothers did.

The President asked, *"How do you know that, Mahadiyi?"*

Mahadiyi replied, *"I know this, Mr. President, for my brother was married to her. My brother was Eko and Indra's father."*

Roger, Sheldon, Idah, the President, and everyone near them kept looking at Mahadiyi, and then at the Suparman brothers. It was pretty evident that they resembled and had similar features.

Mahadiyi then drew his attention toward Eko and Indra and continued, *"Eko, Indra, I am Mahadiyi, your Uncle, your father's brother."*

For the first time ever, Eko and Indra finally had a family. Indra picked up Mahadiyi and raced around Idah, Sheldon, and the President of Indonesia. Idah asked, *"What is all the excitement, Indra?"*

Indra responded, *"This is my Uncle; he just told me. I did not know that Eko and I had an Uncle, our father's brother."*

Sheldon, too, was amused to what he heard and asked right away, *"Hold on a second, what do you mean by 'Uncle?'"*

Roger decided to answer for Mahadiyi and this time, looking into the camera and using a microphone so the crowd could hear, *"This is the man who flew me over the Island. His name is Mahadiyi Suparman, and he is the pilot whom I thought had died. Look closely, and you can see by his eyes and face that he does look like Eko and Indra."* Sheldon was somewhat confused, he was also concerned as there was a possibility of it being a ploy, and a scam to get close to Eko and Indra, or even possibly have bad intentions.

Mahadiyi went on to tell them all about how he had this information, anticipating the expected questions beforehand. Eko and Indra's parents had been dead for nearly twenty years. He described how their mother died, and the kids were lucky to survive.

Their father was distraught over the loss of his wife and decided to leave Indonesia. He was last heard or seen prior to his boat trip to Japan. His boat never arrived, and everyone thought they had no survivors from the shipwreck. The time he mentioned exactly matched Idah's story, verifying the fact that Mahadiyi was not lying. All of what he was saying appeared to be the truth. However, Sheldon was still unsatisfied. He was concerned and wanted more proof rather than just some story claiming that Mahadiyi was actually related to Eko and Indra. All of them were invited back to the President's residence, and Sheldon asked the President if he would allow him to investigate Mahadiyi further to confirm that he had relation and hadn't forged up a story.

The President agreed and asked Sheldon how he planned on attaining satisfactory results. Sheldon replied by claiming that drawing his blood samples and comparing them with Eko and Indra. If their DNA matched, it would prove Mahadiyi's honesty, and if it didn't, then it would conclude that Mahadiyi was being dishonest. Sheldon's team already had Eko and Indra's samples, and all that was to be done was to collect Mahadiyi's.

The President agreed to Sheldon's proposal and advised that test to be conducted both by Indonesian and American doctors to have better results. Other than the President and Sheldon, everyone else was happy about this news, especially Eko, Indra, Idah, and Roger. Roger asked Mahadiyi if he knew about them, to which Mahadiyi responded, *"Yes, Roger, I knew of them. But I thought that the sea had taken them just as the sea took my baby (airplane), my brother and everyone else on the day that he set for the journey along with his motherless twin sons."*

As the bloodwork came back, it was confirmed that what Mahadiyi had said was true; the blood work was indeed a match, and this gave the proof that Eko and Indra had finally found another family member. All of it started making sense as to how the stories of the sumo wrestler justified Eko and Indra's skill. Besides that, they never had any explanation, and all they were left with was amusement. Apparently, this is how they were so tall, standing at eight feet and eight inches.

Sheldon still didn't trust Mahadiyi even after the blood confirmed a match. He figured that there was more to it and was not as convinced as the others were. With the world's greatest current football players to compete against the newly dubbed, *"Emerald of the Equator,"* Sheldon had a lot of time to think.

Chapter 12
Football

Fortunately for Eko and Indra, they started playing football while they were at the compound near Santa Fe. They loved every sport and especially enjoyed playing football. They asked the President, Sheldon, Idah, and a few others from the tribe to stand at the goal line as goalkeepers because they knew that, despite the number of goalkeepers, scoring a goal would be a piece of cake for them. This, too, was to take place with the broadcast being pay-per-view, i.e., anybody who wanted to see a live transmission had to pay to watch these footages in real-time. Only the locals were allowed free entry.

The only guests from anywhere outside of Indonesia were either those who had been with Eko and Indra since the beginning of their journey along with family members from the group of football players who recently joined to partake in this upcoming match. The president of Indonesia, as a symbol of goodwill, announced that the money raised would be offered to help the poor people worldwide. Roger was very happy to hear the announcement. The superstars he had discovered were not just excelling in the sport but were also serving a purpose. Also, Indonesia was not, by any means, a poor country. At least not after the Suparman brothers' contribution. It had all happened in less than a year. Eko and Indra had to put in no effort, and those benefits were phenomenal. Indonesia had revolutionized over a short period of time. It had developed to such an extent that it was then helping countries across the globe. They had made the earth a different place.

All they did was 'play ball.' Mahadiyi, along with his wife, paid Roger a visit when he had invited them over for dinner. Roger loved how simple and welcoming the villagers were to him. He had the same attitude toward meeting everybody, particularly people who were associated with the Suparman brothers in any way. Even if Mahadiyi did appear to be Eko and Indra's relative, his intentions still could never be tested.

Sheldon was only looking for something that would justify his beliefs, but until that was to happen, there wasn't much that he could do. Sheldon wasn't wrong with his approach. With fame and popularity, the threats also increased. Sheldon was in the business for quite some time and had to analyze the risks and ensure their protection.

Roger thought of Mahadiyi completely the opposite of what Sheldon did, for he believed that Mahadiyi was just like Eko, Indra, Idah, and the other villagers, i.e., just like family. This was the first time that Eko and Indra were playing any sports other than baseball in a professional manner.

They played in Santa Fe with the kids; however, no one had seen them play aside from the villagers who were with them at Santa Fe. They were to play against the best football players in the world. The best players were not just from Asia or any particular part of the world, but the best from the whole planet. The greatest current football players playing were excited and ready. This event was bigger than any other event in the world. The funds to be accumulated through the game were predicated to be insanely high.

The pay-per-views had exceeded their previous best and were greater than those that happened for the recent game against the Asian All-Stars Baseball team. The football match had exceeded 3.7 billion purchases. This was to generate a profit of nearly 900 billion dollars that were all to be dedicated to those that were most in need of assistance. The match against the world eleven was, yet again, one-sided. Eko and Indra were unstoppable; they scored one goal after another, and they had almost scored two hundred goals in the first half. The second half was no different.

The match ended at 364-0. They could have scored more, but they were tired of doing the same thing over and over again throughout the game. Instead, they started passing around more and involved other players of their team that were not very skilled in trying something different. The players that were claimed to be the best in the world had been given a crushing defeat by the Indonesian team. The guest team had 365 chances of touching the ball, once when the game began and one every time after a goal was scored.

The moment the opponent team would kick-off, either of the Suparman brothers would get to the ball in an instant, and score at an unstoppable pace. The players of the other team did not even get a chance to intercept, as the Suparman brothers were so quick. Both Eko and Indra scored 182 goals each. They were taking turns and did not miss the target a single time.

The end of the second event was similar to how the first game was. After football and baseball, it was then basketball to be played by the Indonesians against the best athletes in the sport. Even the players who played from the opponent's side were thrilled to play against the Eko and Indra. They were aware that they were playing against these brothers, whose game seemed supernatural. For them, it was an honor to share the same field with the Suparman brothers. The result did not matter to them. Never had any team ever scored as many goals as Eko and Indra individually did. Also, the amount raised had served the cause. Nine hundred billion dollars was raised in a period of a few hours.

The Indonesian president was the first to use these assets productively. This was the first time that Eko and Indra were playing for a purpose aside from generating profits for Sheldon. Idah was pleased to see the boys contribute to social welfare. She even had tears in her eyes when she first heard the president's announcement. Eko and Indra were already everyone's favorite, and this had earned them even more respect. They were geared up to play in the third event, and the hype of it was no less.

After the match, Roger asked Mahadiyi if he, his wife, and Eko and Indra could join him for dinner. He had something that he wanted to give to Mahadiyi, who agreed and felt honored by Roger's invitation. Mahadiyi also admired Roger for the way he treated his nephews. Roger was like a fatherly figure to them and treated them like his children. Mahadiyi had great respect for Roger,and his intentions seemed very pure as they were. If it wasn't for him, the world wouldn't have known Eko and Indra, and neither would have Mahadiyi known about his nephews. Since they were all guests of the President of Indonesia, he had a team assigned to serve the guests over from the United States. The representatives of the President were to ensure that the guests were given the best hospitality and would be served as they pleased. Roger had requested for a vehicle, which was provided as per request. Idah, Susan, and Aspyn also accompanied them.

They got into the van and left the President's residence in complete protocol. The protocol was to stay with them undercover until they reached their destination. The destination chosen was not a populated one as Eko and Indra could be exposed to danger if they were outside, and had public attention. On their way to the place where Roger was taking them, Mahadiyi and his wife told Eko and Indra stories of their parents.

They had so many stories, and the Suparman brothers listened to all of them with great enthusiasm and interest. They were very excited to know about their parents. Prior to Mahadiyi, no one had ever spoken to them about their parents. Hearing the stories made them emotional; it was like they had waited all their lives to know something about their parents. None of the passengers knew where they were going besides Roger. As they got closer to the destination, Mahadiyi had figured out where they were going. He asked Roger with some doubt and then backed up by confidence, *"Roger, are we going where I think we are going?"*

Roger, with a grin, responded, *"And where might that be, Mahadiyi?"*

Mahadiyi answered, *"To where we first met and where I introduce you to my baby?"* Nobody in the van knew what Roger and Mahadiyi were talking about. They just waited eagerly to get there. Roger just smiled and then, after a moment, replied, *"We shall see, Mahadiyi. If I were to tell you, then it wouldn't be a surprise, my friend."* The van pulled into a parking lot, and it was indeed the place Mahadiyi was talking about. It was the place where he and Mahadiyi had met.

Roger opened the door and stepped out. The protocol vehicles had also parked next to the van that they were traveling in. Roger led the way of the group walking through brand new airplanes. One of the airplanes was a twin-engine aircraft, and the other was medium-sized, and the third was the exact same model as Mahadiyi had owned before it went down. Mahadiyi instantly went toward the aircraft that was similar to his, only that it was a brand new version of it, as were the other two airplanes in the hanger. He couldn't believe what he was seeing. Mahadiyi looked at Roger with an excited and emotional smile and asked, *"What is this, Roger?"*

Roger took a step closer to him and said, *"Mahadiyi, this is my gift to you."*

Nothing could have made Mahadiyi as happy as he was then, *"You got me my baby back, Roger! Only that she is newer than my last baby."*

Roger told Mahadiyi where he recovered the plane from and that Mahadiyi had guessed it right. Mahadiyi then only thought that Roger had gifted him a plane. It was partially correct as it wasn't a plane, but rather planes that were gifted to him. Roger then told him then that all the three planes were a present from him to Mahadiyi.

Roger stated, *"Well, Mahadiyi. I didn't just get you your baby back. I, or I mean, we, as in everyone here, we all decided to get you these three planes here. They are yours, all three of them, a gift from all of us."*

Eko then joined the conversation, *"Uncle Mahadiyi, we also bought you this building... they call it a hanger."*

Indra added, *"And we bought you the house for you and your wife,"* pointing toward a house that was nearby.

Mahadiyi and his wife began to cry. Tears of happiness started dripping down their cheeks. Idah looking at Roger, said, *"Roger, I remember that day when you were crying, and you said they were tears of joy. I see that happening again today."*

Mahadiyi and his wife were at a loss for words. It was evident that they were filled with joy and were very thankful. Sometimes words are not required, and expressions are sufficient for heart-to-heart communication. Mahadiyi then invited all of them to join him and his wife for the first meal at their new residence. Eko asked his uncle, *"How about we all go for a flight in your new plane, Uncle Mahadiyi?"*

Mahadiyi, who was more than happy, agreed. They all got into the twin jet for their flight. Roger looked at Mahadiyi and said, *"Well, Mahadiyi, this is one of your new babies, but I have told you that she won't take us to the moon."* All of them laughed, *"Emeralds of the Equator is what I will call my new babies,"* Mahadiyi commented as they   took   off.

Chapter 13
Basketball

The opposing team consisted of the top fifteen best basketball players in the entire world. The world had seen what had happened in the two previous contests, and now it was time for them to see it for themselves. Even scoring a single basket was going to be impossible. When a team was playing against Eko and Indra, it was the hardest thing that any of these basketball players had ever faced at any point in time throughout their lives. Yet, the basketball players did not worry about losing to Eko and Indra. Instead, they hoped to exceed the pay-per-views, just like the football game.

They hoped to exceed trillion dollars to help the needy people, just like those that played against Eko and Indra in the football match. Nothing was more satisfactory than to be part of a cause. By this time, the pay-per-views were nearly 4.8 billion. As was the case in the earlier contests, the people of Indonesia were allowed free access. All of the money earned was to be used to improve the poorest of the poor and was expected to help those in need from every part of the world. The opposing basketball team had the cream of basketball players.

They were warming up. Generally, every basketball stadium in the world has a capacity of less than twenty thousand. However, in the stadiums where these contests were taking place had capacity tenfold more than other stadiums. Every person in the world wanted to see the live streaming of the game. It was a huge platform to be a part of, regardless of whether the game was to be completely one-sided; the exposure and outreach was undoubtedly unmatchable.

When the home team joined the guests at the practice sessions, they were amazed by the height of both Eko and Indra. They could easily dunk a basketball without having the need to jump. The other members of the home team could barely score a basket, but they all knew that much similar to the previous games, the other members of the home team were only there to comply with the rules and regulations. The players of both the teams greeted each other before the game. The players of the visiting team also took pictures with them. They weren't there for winning. For the players of the world basketball team, victory was being part of the team.

Being in the team, they acknowledged the fact that they were the best in the game and that they had the potential to win against any team of the world with the exception that neither of the Suparman brothers played. Even if one of them was on the opponent side, giving a tough competition was impossible, let alone winning it. As it was in the previous games of baseball and football, technology was used. In this game, they used the same nanotechnology that was used in the baseball season.

However, because of the fouls, they did require officials to be present for the human calls of any fouls or violations. They were all formalities because the ball was only to stay with Eko and Indra, and to foul them was just as difficult as it was going to be for scoring. Since the results were already predicted, and the members of the other team stood no chance of participating in the game besides showing their presence in the court, a different regulation was introduced exclusively for it.

This was the final contest, and everyone was expecting the same results as they had witnessed in baseball and football. Yet, to make it fair, they decided that only Eko or

Indra would take turns rotating in and out of the lineup and that neither would be on the basketball court at the same time together. Even with just one playing at a time, the competition did not get any easier for the opponents. Each of the two had the ability to run faster than race cars, and the results were the same as they had always been in all sporting contests they participated in. They easily kept on scoring, while the opponents struggled and failed to get any ball possession. The only competition they had was scoring more points than each other. Since their skills and techniques were exactly the same, they always managed to match each other's performance, and so they did in the basketball game.

After two-quarters of the match, the score was 206 points for the home team, and there were no points scored by the guest team. There was nothing different in the final two quarters, and the game ended with the Indonesian Basketball Team scoring 412 points, while the world's greatest basketball team was not scoring a single point. Eko and Indra were undoubtedly the World's Greatest, not just in baseball, but also in Football and Basketball. There was not even a single sport in which they were not good. Every person who watched them play was blown away from their talent, and despite being the results very predictable and constant, the interest of the masses never decreased.

There was a fantastic closing ceremony that was attended by the President of the United States as the chief guest. The closing ceremony had singing performances from the national singers of Indonesia. Prior to the fireworks that were officially the last activity of the events, Eko and Indra were interviewed. They were being watched live by billions of people, including the ones present in the stadium.

Eko was asked about what their plans were for the future. Eko responded that they were going to participate in next year's Summer Olympics. To his answer, a loud cheer went up in the crowd. They were glad that they were going to get another opportunity to watch the Suparman brothers perform. Also, on the next occasion, they were going to take part in activities they had never performed before.

It was obvious that there wasn't any training required. All they had to know was the rules on which they could produce extraordinary results. They had already broken every statistical records in the baseball section, and now it was time to have other sports sections dominated by their names. It should be noted that Indonesia had never taken part in the Olympics before with great success.

In the roar of the crowd, the only person that was not thrilled by the answer was Sheldon. He said to himself, *"Compete in the Summer Olympics?"*

Sheldon knew this was going to happen but subconsciously hoped that it didn't. This meant that, in the next season of Major League Baseball, his key players were to miss some of the games. Even though they would still be the champions if Eko and Indra managed to play even half of the games, yet, as the owner of the baseball club, he was worried.

Sheldon was wise enough to know that it was best to keep it to himself, and by no means did Sheldon wish to upset Eko or Indra. After all, they helped him to accomplish something far greater than Sheldon had ever thought or hoped. Even though Sheldon had put in all of the money and effort to have them on board; however, if he wouldn't have done so, someone else might have.

Without the Suparman brothers, Sheldon could never have become what he was now. In terms of wealth, Sheldon was now the richest person in the world, for the Conquistadors were now worth over a trillion dollars alone. The merchandise for the Conquistadors was sold faster than they could be made. Conquistadors were awarded a prize of honor by the Baseball federation for contributing to the growth of the game and discovering the best players of all time. The popularity and wealth earned by Sheldon hadn't left him in any moral position to make it difficult for Suparman brothers to follow their dreams. They had the right to follow their hearts, and serving their country was something they were very passionate about.

Eko and Indra, on the other hand, were raised by a fine woman. Idah had groomed them as men of honor. They respected every person they met regardless of their age or designation. Their attitude with the President and the chauffeur was the same. Even when stardom hit them, they never disobeyed Idah; neither did their attitude change.

They still had the same mindset, the one that they had at the village. The only difference was that, back then, nobody knew them. Now, they were the favorites of the entire world. The systems used to officiate the baseball games, which was such a huge success that all other sports were updating and modernizing their respective sport. Since the technology was created by Sheldon's tech specialist, he earned billions of dollars through its implementation.

Nanotechnology had become the largest business worldwide and had perfected decision-making aspects, thereby improving the overall quality of the game by promoting fair play as much as it possibly could be done. The nanotechnology was part of horse races, NASCAR, ice hockey, and simply any other sports. The credit of this transformation was also to Eko and Indra. If it wasn't for them, the ease caused by the integration of this technology would have never been noticeable, and the world would not have shifted to technology-based reviewer systems.

Nanotechnology was to be used in the winter and Summer Olympics as well in the near future. This industry was even bigger than in the late 1990's internet boom. Its demand was increasing by the day. There was a single vendor of this technology in the market, and it was nobody other than Sheldon. Since the inclusion of Eko and Indra in Sheldon's life, everything he touched turned to gold.

Sheldon was not the only one who benefitted; he was one of the many who did. They managed to transform the whole of Indonesia from a developing economy to a superpower. It was the richest country in the world.

A decade ago, no one could have guessed that Indonesia would lead the world in economy and wealth. The funds raised through the last three events alone had exceeded the collections of any organization or government in terms of social service. Eko and Indra had, in less than a year, changed the entire world for the better. Those who were hungry or even thirsty now had the means to eat and drink clean water.

Others that needed a home or shelter were now no longer homeless. Education was provided for everyone to ensure that the work they started would last for generations. Anyone ill was no longer turned away for not having the money. Anybody who needed medical help was provided with it. The world faced great improvements because of Eko and Indra.

Idah never thought that they were capable of making such a significant difference. She was proud to have mothered them and raised them up as men who were changing the world positively. Roger would have tears in his eyes whenever he would realize the difference the boys had created in the world. Baseball was just a little segment of their lives. The bigger picture was that they had an impact on every aspect of mankind. *"I never knew that these kids would do such wonders,"* Roger often said to Idah. *"Neither did I,"* she always replied.

Often, when they ran into a reporter, whether was Eko, Indra, Roger, or Sheldon, they always gave Idah full credit. Idah deserved respect; she had given up everything for her people, and the next thing she wanted was to make sure that they helped millions of others. They had both the resources and ability to do those things, which they eventually did.

It was hard to find a place across the globe that did not have sports complexes and fields where ordinary people could go and play. Every sport was promoted, and every basic necessity was available in the civilized world.

Chapter 14
No Wonder

The news given by Mahadiyi had explained a lot about Eko and Indra. Since their popularity had greatly increased, many historians had started researching the Suparman brothers. They had learned quite a bit about the Sumo Family. They were linked back to Japanese history, and, with time, Mahadiyi's claims only appeared to be true. The season had completed, and so had the contests in Indonesia.

It was now time for Eko, Indra, and the other members of their village to spend some time together. Even though they were still uncertain of their home, they wanted to spend some quality time together. That's all the villagers had wanted since the beginning of the journey, including. They wanted to live in peace just as they did before moving to the States.

They enjoyed the games and the success of their family, but after a point in time, they were overwhelmed. The secret location of Santa Fe, New Mexico, where they were accommodated by Sheldon throughout the season, was no more secretive. Sheldon and Roger both realized that they needed to provide for them a place they could call home. Now that their island was no longer available, they needed a place that was home for them. Nike had agreed to make arrangements for them to leave the island, but Idah had decided that a new place was needed, which no one knew about. She thought that it was the best for the villagers and her adopted children since the home was supposed to be a place where they lived with a peaceful mind.

After all, money, wealth, and the comforts of living a life in luxury were not what any of the villagers wanted or desired. They were simple people and found happiness spending time with each other. The life they knew and experienced long before the Suparman brothers became sensations was simple and peaceful. The stardom is not what attracted them. Family was their topmost priority, and the fame had sabotaged it to a great degree.

Everybody had benefited significantly through their association. Sheldon had a net worth of over a trillion dollars. Roger had himself become a billionaire. Indonesia, as a state, prospered due to the Suparman brothers. This was just the beginning of their journey. After the mutual consent, Roger and Sheldon, on Idah's proposition, decided to find a new place for the villagers. They had to ensure that the place was very remote and hidden from everyone else besides the villagers. Barbara was always an integral part of Sheldon's business. She was responsible for purchasing locations such as remote islands and all possible places where the people of the village, along with Eko and Indra, could live in isolation. Eko and Indra had also become quite wealthy. However, they never worried or were even concerned about money or wealth. The group began searching for a rightful place with full priority.

They looked out for new places that could be home for them all. They visited every potential place to ensure if it was suitable for the villagers as per Idah's suggestions. It was a very interesting project as they had somewhat started welfare work. They did so by helping anyone they came across in the process. Since they were looking for a remote area, they focused on underdeveloped locations, and every time they found one, they ensured that they improved their standard of living. This was irrespective of the fact that if the place was or was not suitable, they still did help the people living, thereby providing them with utilities that were scarcely available.

Roger focused on building schools and sports complexes. Every place they visited was transformed into a different and better place when they left. Because of all the wealth they had generated, they were able to help millions and millions of people throughout the entire world. The places that were underdeveloped and had no sports were all developed by Roger and Sheldon to the degree that baseball, football, and basketball could all be played there. This allowed children as well as adults to be part of these sports. Education was the most important aspect, and Idah decided that she wanted all of these places to have better schools and took the responsibility of taking care of the education of the places they visited.

To find a place that was remote and suitable for the villagers was a very difficult task. It had been over a month and a half of searching and visiting when they finally found a place. This place was a large island that was not populated at all. The island was very near to Australia and lay close to its eastern side. Eko and Indra had spent all their lives by the ocean, and the island was indeed very suitable for them to accept as home. The night on the island was very similar to the ones they had on the Indonesian island. The sky was full of stars that reminded them of the place they called home. The freshness of the moist air and the isolated atmosphere had brought a smile on the faces of all the villagers. By this time, it was evident that Eko and Susan had fallen in love. So was the case with Indra and Aspyn. They had developed a great understanding and spent most of the time together. Roger and Idah had noticed their growing interest. Roger suggested to Idah that it was indeed an ideal time for them to get married. They couldn't be certain for how long the place was to stay secretive, and before that happened, it was only smart to get them married.

Idah couldn't have agreed more. It was a custom of their tribe to marry at a young age, and so she agreed to Roger's advice. Eko and Indra were very excited to see their new home. They built their huts identical to the ones they lived in at the island where Roger had found them. This reflected how money was not what they wanted, but home. They did not make a fancy home that had expensive décor, but they built a hut that resembled their simplicity. It was decided that the first night they were to live in their new huts, they would sleep as married men. It was time for Eko and Susan's wedding, along with Indra and Aspyn's.

The wedding had no outsiders; it couldn't have had any as this would have made the place public. It was only the people of the village along with Sheldon, Roger, Barbara, Ron, Bill, Jeff, Malhadyi, and his wife. They were the only people present at the wedding that were not part of the village. The wedding day had come, and there was nothing royal about it since the brothers were quite simple. All they wanted was their family, and they were glad to be accompanied by them. Eko and Indra were finally husbands to Susan and Aspyn, respectively. They had long waited for it and were glad to have married the women they had fallen in love with.

They say that the matches are made in heaven. Susan and Aspyn were no different from Eko and Indra. They had no interest in living a life like most women of their generation. They were born and raised in America but were very different. They did not dream of living a life that was large and full of comforts. They did not want to live as rich people did. They enjoyed spending time with Eko and Indra without any regard to the location or luxuries. They had developed a good relationship with the villagers and had become a part of the village family.

The villagers admired these American women and had accepted them with happiness and love. All of the villagers loved Susan and Aspyn and were glad that Eko and Indra had found wives for themselves. Susan and Aspyn were as much a part of the village as Eko and Indra. They couldn't imagine life without their new family. They loved their new home and family. Even though they had the money to live anywhere they wished for, all they wanted was to live with Eko and Indra. Their happiness lied in the happiness of their husbands. They were just as glad as their husbands because they had married the men they were deeply in love with, and as marriage is stated a new beginning, it had started amazingly.

Eko and Indra decided that they were going to miss the second season of the upcoming baseball season and maybe not even defend their World Series Championship. They had been in the news for a very long time, and it was something that they weren't used to. Nobody knew them a year ago, and now they were the most famous people in the world. Sheldon wasn't thrilled at all with that decision. He wanted them to play, but he did not want to force them in any manner. Sheldon knew that without Eko and Indra, he would have never won the season so comfortably.

The figures of his bank account had multiplied since the inclusion of the Suparman brothers, and he couldn't have achieved any of it without them. They raised over $2.5 trillion for those in need. The Albuquerque Conquistadors had a perfect season and were the defending champions. The world was a far better place than it ever had been prior to Eko and Indra. Their impact was global, and the world had become an entirely different place.

The newly wedded couples had decided to start a family, and it made Idah proud, thinking of how her boys were turning into men. Roger had also developed a strong bond with the boys and was extremely happy to find out that both his recruits were on the verge of becoming fathers. Both Susan and Aspyn were expecting. Interestingly, not only were they expecting a child, but also twins. They were both very excited, and so were their husbands.

The Summer Olympics were round the corner, and Eko and Indra were eager to participate. They wanted to do something different, and the Olympics was an ideal platform for them. The President of Indonesia was quite pleased to have them participate while representing

Indonesia. They were learning about the different Summer Olympic events that they could compete in.

Everyone was to gain something out of it. Sheldon's dream of winning the second season had collapsed since the Suparman brothers were not participating, and winning the season without them was an extremely difficult task. Nevertheless, he was to earn additional business for the Nanotechnology. Wherever Eko and Indra were to participate, modernization of the equipment was necessary. This is why both the Winter and Summer Olympics were to be upgraded with Sheldon's equipment. Indonesia was the top favorite country in the Summer Olympic Medal Counts with Eko and Indra training in many different events.

Eko, Indra, and the entire village were waiting for the inclusion of four more members to the family, with both Susan and Aspyn being pregnant with twins. The future couldn't have seemed any better. They were finally living in peace and had to face no disturbance from any of the media and the fans, as the world was unaware of the location of their new home. The future of the tribe looked bright, with the addition of four children. It was very promising, and after making their way through the

Indonesian island, they were undisputedly the best athletes in the world. Everything happens for a reason.

If the plane had not crashed, Roger would have never made it to the island, and the Suparman brothers were to remain undiscovered. Sheldon offered Roger a scouting job when the world had turned its back on him, and it did pay back amazingly well. The world knew about Eko and Indra, but this was the beginning of a journey. There was still a long way to go.

The Next adenture will be "Eko and Indra: The Summer Olympians."

ROGER SCHAFER

Bibliography

1936 Baseball Hall of Fame balloting. (2018). In *Wikipedia.* Retrieved from https://en.wikipedia.org/w/index.php?title=1936_Baseball_Hall_of_Fame_balloting HYPERLINK "https://en.wikipedia.org/w/index.php?title=1936_Baseball_Hall_of_Fame_balloting&oldid=873439453"& HYPERLINK "https://en.wikipedia.org/w/index.php?title=1936_Baseball_Hall_of_Fame_balloting&oldid=873439453"oldid=873439453

2006 World Baseball Classic. (2019). In *Wikipedia.* Retrieved from https://en.wikipedia.org/w/index.php?title=2006_World_Baseball_Classic HYPERLINK "https://en.wikipedia.org/w/index.php?title=2006_World_Baseball_Classic&oldid=877461051"& HYPERLINK "https://en.wikipedia.org/w/index.php?title=2006_World_Baseball_Classic&oldid=877461051"oldid=877461051

2008 Summer Olympics. (2019). In *Wikipedia.* Retrieved from https://en.wikipedia.org/w/index.php?title=2008_Summer_Olympics HYPERLINK "https://en.wikipedia.org/w/index.php?title=

2008_Summer_Olympics&oldid=87971808
8"&   HYPERLINK
"https://en.wikipedia.org/w/index.php?title=
2008_Summer_Olympics&oldid=87971808
8"oldid=879718088

2011 Baseball World Cup. (2018). In *Wikipedia*.
Retrieved   from
https://en.wikipedia.org/w/index.php?title=2
011_Ba   HYPERLINK
"https://en.wikipedia.org/w/index.php?title=
2011_Baseball_World_Cup&oldid=869090
555"seball_World_Cup   HYPERLINK
"https://en.wikipedia.org/w/index.php?title=
2011_Baseball_World_Cup&oldid=869090
555"&   HYPERLINK
"https://en.wikipedia.org/w/index.php?title=
2011_Baseball_World_Cup&oldid=869090
555"oldid=869090555

2012 Summer Olympics. (2019). In *Wikipedia*.
Retrieved   from
https://en.wikipedia.org/w/index.php?title=2
012_Summer_Olympics   HYPERLINK
"https://en.wikipedia.org/w/index.php?title=
2012_Summer_Olympics&oldid=88038054
9"&   HYPERLINK
"https://en.wikipedia.org/w/index.php?title=
2012_Summer_Olympics&oldid=88038054
9"oldid=880380549

A Little Pretty Pocket-Book. (2019). In *Wikipedia*. Retrieved from https://en.wikipedia.org/w/index.php?title= A_Little_Pretty_Pocket-Book HYPERLINK "https://en.wikipedia.org/w/index.php?title= A_Little_Pretty_Pocket-Book&oldid=880046031"& HYPERLINK "https://en.wikipedia.org/w/index.php?title= A_Little_Pretty_Pocket-Book&oldid=880046031"oldid=880046031

Alexander Cartwright. (2018). In *Wikipedia*. Retrieved from https://en.wikipedia.org/w/index.php?title= Alexander_Cartwright HYPERLINK "https://en.wikipedia.org/w/index.php?title= Alexander_Cartwright&oldid=874040968" & HYPERLINK "https://en.wikipedia.org/w/index.php?title= Alexander_Cartwright&oldid=874040968"o ldid=874040968

Babe Ruth. (2019). In *Wikipedia*. Retrieved from https://en.wikipedia.org/w/index.php?title=B abe_Ruth HYPERLINK "https://en.wikipedia.org/w/index.php?title= Babe_Ruth&oldid=881075944"& HYPERLINK "https://en.wikipedia.org/w/index.php?title= Babe_Ruth&oldid=881075944"oldid=88107 5944

Baseball at the Summer Olympics. (2019). In *Wikipedia*. Retrieved from https://en.wikipedia.org/w/index.php?title=B aseball_at_the_Summer_Olympics HYPERLINK "https://en.wikipedia.org/w/index.php?title= Baseball_at_the_Summer_Olympics&oldid =876793890"& HYPERLINK "https://en.wikipedia.org/w/index.php?title= Baseball_at_the_Summer_Olympics&oldid =876793890"oldid=876793890

Baseball Before We Knew It. (2018). In *Wikipedia*. Retrieved from https://en.wikipedia.org/w/index.php?title=B aseball_Before_We_Knew_It HYPERLINK "https://en.wikipedia.org/w/index.php?title= Baseball_Before_We_Knew_It&oldid=8390 62647"& HYPERLINK "https://en.wikipedia.org/w/index.php?title= Baseball_Before_We_Knew_It&oldid=8390 62647"oldid=839062647

Baseball in Japan. (2019). In *Wikipedia*. Retrieved from https://en.wikipedia.org/w/index.php?title=B aseball_in_Japan HYPERLINK "https://en.wikipedia.org/w/index.php?title= Baseball_in_Japan&oldid=878819385"& HYPERLINK "https://en.wikipedia.org/w/index.php?title=

Baseball_in_Japan&oldid=878819385"oldid=878819385

Baseball in South Korea. (2018). In *Wikipedia*. Retrieved from https://en.wikipedia.org/w/index.php?title=Baseball_in_South_Korea HYPERLINK "https://en.wikipedia.org/w/index.php?title=Baseball_in_South_Korea&oldid=874551118"& HYPERLINK "https://en.wikipedia.org/w/index.php?title=Baseball_in_South_Korea&oldid=874551118"oldid=874551118

Baseball in Venezuela. (2018). In *Wikipedia*. Retrieved from https://en.wikipedia.org/w/index.php?title=Baseball_in_Venezuela HYPERLINK "https://en.wikipedia.org/w/index.php?title=Baseball_in_Venezuela&oldid=863696864"& HYPERLINK "https://en.wikipedia.org/w/index.php?title=Baseball_in_Venezuela&oldid=863696864"oldid=863696864

Baseball World Cup. (2019). In *Wikipedia*. Retrieved from https://en.wikipedia.org/w/index.php?title=Baseball_World_Cup HYPERLINK "https://en.wikipedia.org/w/index.php?title=Baseball_World_Cup&oldid=880207679"& HYPERLINK

"https://en.wikipedia.org/w/index.php?title=
Baseball_World_Cup&oldid=880207679"ol
did=880207679

Bat-and-ball games. (2018). In *Wikipedia*. Retrieved
from
https://en.wikipedia.org/w/index.php?title=B
at-and-ball_games   HYPERLINK
"https://en.wikipedia.org/w/index.php?title=
Bat-and-ball_games&oldid=861975432"&
HYPERLINK
"https://en.wikipedia.org/w/index.php?title=
Bat-and-
ball_games&oldid=861975432"oldid=86197
5432

Batting (baseball). (2019). In *Wikipedia*. Retrieved from
https://en.wikipedia.org/w/index.php?title=B
atting_(baseball)   HYPERLINK
"https://en.wikipedia.org/w/index.php?title=
Batting_(baseball)&oldid=878619079"&
HYPERLINK
"https://en.wikipedia.org/w/index.php?title=
Batting_(baseball)&oldid=878619079"oldid
=878619079

Caribbean Series. (2019). In *Wikipedia*. Retrieved from
https://en.wikipedia.org/w/index.php?title=C
aribbean_Series   HYPERLINK
"https://en.wikipedia.org/w/index.php?title=
Caribbean_Series&oldid=881232556"&
HYPERLINK

"https://en.wikipedia.org/w/index.php?title=
Caribbean_Series&oldid=881232556"oldid=
881232556

China. (2019). In *Wikipedia*. Retrieved from
https://en.wikipedia.org/w/index.php?title=C
hina HYPERLINK
"https://en.wikipedia.org/w/index.php?title=
China&oldid=881730477"& HYPERLINK
"https://en.wikipedia.org/w/index.php?title=
China&oldid=881730477"oldid=881730477

Dead-ball era. (2019). In *Wikipedia*. Retrieved from
https://en.wikipedia.org/w/index.php?title=
Dead-ball_era HYPERLINK
"https://en.wikipedia.org/w/index.php?title=
Dead-ball_era&oldid=879281048"&
HYPERLINK
"https://en.wikipedia.org/w/index.php?title=
Dead-
ball_era&oldid=879281048"oldid=8792810
48

Dominican Professional Baseball League. (2019). In
Wikipedia. Retrieved from
https://en.wikipedia.org/w/index.php?title=
Dominican_Professional_Baseball_League
HYPERLINK
"https://en.wikipedia.org/w/index.php?title=
Dominican_Professional_Baseball_League
&oldid=879903006"& HYPERLINK
"https://en.wikipedia.org/w/index.php?title=

Dominican_Professional_Baseball_League
&oldid=879903006"oldid=879903006

Farm team. (2018). In *Wikipedia*. Retrieved from
https://en.wikipedia.org/w/index.php?title=F
arm_team   HYPERLINK
"https://en.wikipedia.org/w/index.php?title=
Farm_team&oldid=829242369"&
HYPERLINK
"https://en.wikipedia.org/w/index.php?title=
Farm_team&oldid=829242369"oldid=82924
2369

Frederick, Prince of Wales. (2019). In *Wikipedia*.
Retrieved   from
https://en.wikipedia.org/w/index.php?title=F
rederick,_Prince_of_Wales   HYPERLINK
"https://en.wikipedia.org/w/index.php?title=
Frederick,_Prince_of_Wales&oldid=881822
981"&   HYPERLINK
"https://en.wikipedia.org/w/index.php?title=
Frederick,_Prince_of_Wales&oldid=881822
981"oldid=881822981

General manager (baseball). (2018). In *Wikipedia*.
Retrieved   from
https://en.wikipedia.org/w/index.php?title=
General_manager_(baseball) HYPERLINK
"https://en.wikipedia.org/w/index.php?title=
General_manager_(baseball)&oldid=833052
010"&   HYPERLINK
"https://en.wikipedia.org/w/index.php?title=

General_manager_(baseball)&oldid=833052
010"oldid=833052010

History of baseball in the United States. (2019). In
Wikipedia. Retrieved from
https://en.wikipedia.org/w/index.php?title=
History_of_baseball_in_the_United_States
HYPERLINK
"https://en.wikipedia.org/w/index.php?title=
History_of_baseball_in_the_United_States&
oldid=881616810"& HYPERLINK
"https://en.wikipedia.org/w/index.php?title=
History_of_baseball_in_the_United_States&
oldid=881616810"oldid=881616810

Hoboken, New Jersey. (2019). In *Wikipedia*. Retrieved
from
https://en.wikipedia.org/w/index.php?title=
Hoboken,_New_Jersey HYPERLINK
"https://en.wikipedia.org/w/index.php?title=
Hoboken,_New_Jersey&oldid=879473582"
& HYPERLINK
"https://en.wikipedia.org/w/index.php?title=
Hoboken,_New_Jersey&oldid=879473582"
oldid=879473582

International Association for Professional Base Ball
Players. (2018). In *Wikipedia*. Retrieved
from
https://en.wikipedia.org/w/index.php?title=I
nternational_Association_for_Professional_
Base_Ball_Play HYPERLINK

"https://en.wikipedia.org/w/index.php?title=
International_Association_for_Professional_
Base_Ball_Players&oldid=846678651"ers
HYPERLINK
"https://en.wikipedia.org/w/index.php?title=
International_Association_for_Professional_
Base_Ball_Players&oldid=846678651"&
HYPERLINK
"https://en.wikipedia.org/w/index.php?title=
International_Association_for_Professional_
Base_Ball_Players&oldid=846678651"oldid
=846678651

International Baseball Federation. (2018a). In
Wikipedia. Retrieved from
https://en.wikipedia.org/w/index.php?title=I
nternational_Baseball_Federation
HYPERLINK
"https://en.wikipedia.org/w/index.php?title=
International_Baseball_Federation&oldid=8
67283095"& HYPERLINK
"https://en.wikipedia.org/w/index.php?title=
International_Baseball_Federation&oldid=8
67283095"oldid=867283095

International Baseball Federation. (2018). In *Wikipedia.*
Retrieved from
https://en.wikipedia.org/w/index.php?title=I
nternational_Baseball_Federation
HYPERLINK
"https://en.wikipedia.org/w/index.php?title=
International_Baseball_Federation&oldid=8

67283095"&   HYPERLINK
"https://en.wikipedia.org/w/index.php?title=
International_Baseball_Federation&oldid=8
67283095"oldid=867283095

International Olympic Committee. (2019). In *Wikipedia*.
Retrieved   from
https://en.wikipedia.org/w/index.php?title=I
nternational_Olympic_Committee
HYPERLINK
"https://en.wikipedia.org/w/index.php?title=
International_Olympic_Committee&oldid=8
80971732"&   HYPERLINK
"https://en.wikipedia.org/w/index.php?title=
International_Olympic_Committee&oldid=8
80971732"oldid=880971732

International Softball Federation. (2018). In *Wikipedia*.
Retrieved   from
https://en.wikipedia.org/w/index.php?title=I
nternational_Softball_Federation
HYPERLINK
"https://en.wikipedia.org/w/index.php?title=
International_Softball_Federation&oldid=85
8912454"&   HYPERLINK
"https://en.wikipedia.org/w/index.php?title=
International_Softball_Federation&oldid=85
8912454"oldid=858912454

Italian Baseball League. (2018). In *Wikipedia*. Retrieved
from
https://en.wikipedia.org/w/index.php?title=It

alian_Baseball_League   HYPERLINK
"https://en.wikipedia.org/w/index.php?title=
Italian_Baseball_League&oldid=858423060
"&   HYPERLINK
"https://en.wikipedia.org/w/index.php?title=
Italian_Baseball_League&oldid=858423060
"oldid=858423060

John Newbery. (2019). In *Wikipedia*. Retrieved from
https://en.wikipedia.org/w/index.php?title=J
ohn_Newbery   HYPERLINK
"https://en.wikipedia.org/w/index.php?title=
John_Newbery&oldid=877260652"&
HYPERLINK
"https://en.wikipedia.org/w/index.php?title=
John_Newbery&oldid=877260652"oldid=87
7260652

Knickerbocker Club. (2018). In *Wikipedia*. Retrieved
from
https://en.wikipedia.org/w/index.php?title=
Knickerbocker_Club   HYPERLINK
"https://en.wikipedia.org/w/index.php?title=
Knickerbocker_Club&oldid=872737847"&
HYPERLINK
"https://en.wikipedia.org/w/index.php?title=
Knickerbocker_Club&oldid=872737847"old
id=872737847

Knickerbocker Rules. (2017). In *Wikipedia*. Retrieved
from
https://en.wikipedia.org/w/index.php?title=

Knickerbocker_Rules   HYPERLINK
"https://en.wikipedia.org/w/index.php?title=
Knickerbocker_Rules&oldid=786140933"&
HYPERLINK
"https://en.wikipedia.org/w/index.php?title=
Knickerbocker_Rules&oldid=786140933"ol
did=786140933

Liga de Béisbol Profesional Roberto Clemente. (2019).
In *Wikipedia*. Retrieved from
https://en.wikipedia.org/w/index.php?title=L
iga_de_B%C3%A9isbol_Profesional_Rober
to_Clemente   HYPERLINK
"https://en.wikipedia.org/w/index.php?title=
Liga_de_B%C3%A9isbol_Profesional_Rob
erto_Clemente&oldid=880273976"&
HYPERLINK
"https://en.wikipedia.org/w/index.php?title=
Liga_de_B%C3%A9isbol_Profesional_Rob
erto_Clemente&oldid=880273976"oldid=88
0273976

Little League Baseball. (2019). In *Wikipedia*. Retrieved
from
https://en.wikipedia.org/w/index.php?title=L
ittle_League_Baseball   HYPERLINK
"https://en.wikipedia.org/w/index.php?title=
Little_League_Baseball&oldid=880209543"
&   HYPERLINK
"https://en.wikipedia.org/w/index.php?title=
Little_League_Baseball&oldid=880209543"
oldid=880209543

Mexican Pacific League. (2019). In *Wikipedia.* Retrieved from https://en.wikipedia.org/w/index.php?title= Mexican_Pacific_League HYPERLINK "https://en.wikipedia.org/w/index.php?title= Mexican_Pacific_League&oldid=88074296 6"& HYPERLINK "https://en.wikipedia.org/w/index.php?title= Mexican_Pacific_League&oldid=88074296 6"oldid=880742966

Montreal Expos. (2019). In *Wikipedia.* Retrieved from https://en.wikipedia.org/w/index.php?title= Montreal_Expos HYPERLINK "https://en.wikipedia.org/w/index.php?title= Montreal_Expos&oldid=881776997"& HYPERLINK "https://en.wikipedia.org/w/index.php?title= Montreal_Expos&oldid=881776997"oldid= 881776997

National Baseball Hall of Fame and Museum. (2019). In *Wikipedia.* Retrieved from https://en.wikipedia.org/w/index.php?title= National HYPERLINK "https://en.wikipedia.org/w/index.php?title= National_Baseball_Hall_of_Fame_and_Mus eum&oldid=880192949"_Baseball_Hall_of _Fame_and_Museum HYPERLINK "https://en.wikipedia.org/w/index.php?title= National_Baseball_Hall_of_Fame_and_Mus eum&oldid=880192949"& HYPERLINK

"https://en.wikipedia.org/w/index.php?title=
National_Baseball_Hall_of_Fame_and_Mus
eum&oldid=880192949"oldid=880192949

National sport. (2019). In *Wikipedia*. Retrieved from
https://en.wikipedia.org/w/index.php?title=
National_sport   HYPERLINK
"https://en.wikipedia.org/w/index.php?title=
National_sport&oldid=881685092"&
HYPERLINK
"https://en.wikipedia.org/w/index.php?title=
National_sport&oldid=881685092"oldid=88
1685092

Negro American League. (2019). In *Wikipedia*.
Retrieved   from
https://en.wikipedia.org/w/index.php?title=
Negro_American_League   HYPERLINK
"https://en.wikipedia.org/w/index.php?title=
Negro_American_League&oldid=88154990
0"&   HYPERLINK
"https://en.wikipedia.org/w/index.php?title=
Negro_American_League&oldid=88154990
0"oldid=881549900

Negro National League (1933–1948). (2019). In
Wikipedia.   Retrieved   from
https://en.wikipedia.org/w/index.php?title=
Negro_National_League_(1933%E2%80%9
31948)   HYPERLINK
"https://en.wikipedia.org/w/index.php?title=
Negro_National_League_(1933%E2%80%9

31948)&oldid=877820508"& HYPERLINK "https://en.wikipedia.org/w/index.php?title= Negro_National_League_(1933%E2%80%9 31948)&oldid=877820508"oldid=87782050 8

New York Knickerbockers. (2019). In *Wikipedia*. Retrieved from https://en.wikipedia.org/w/index.php?title= New_Yo HYPERLINK "https://en.wikipedia.org/w/index.php?title= New_York_Knickerbockers&oldid=880567 033"rk_Knickerbockers HYPERLINK "https://en.wikipedia.org/w/index.php?title= New_York_Knickerbockers&oldid=880567 033"& HYPERLINK "https://en.wikipedia.org/w/index.php?title= New_York_Knickerbockers&oldid=880567 033"oldid=880567033

Olympic sports. (2019). In *Wikipedia*. Retrieved from https://en.wikipedia.org/w/index.php?title= Olympic_sports HYPERLINK "https://en.wikipedia.org/w/index.php?title= Olympic_sports&oldid=877500861"& HYPERLINK "https://en.wikipedia.org/w/index.php?title= Olympic_sports&oldid=877500861"oldid=8 77500861

South Korea. (2019). In *Wikipedia*. Retrieved from https://en.wikipedia.org/w/index.php?title=S

outh_Korea HYPERLINK "https://en.wikipedia.org/w/index.php?title= South_Korea&oldid=881558515"& HYPERLINK "https://en.wikipedia.org/w/index.php?title= South_Korea&oldid=881558515"oldid=881 558515

St. Louis Cardinals. (2019). In *Wikipedia*. Retrieved from https://en.wikipedia.org/w/index.php?title=S t._Louis_Cardinals HYPERLINK "https://en.wikipedia.org/w/index.php?title= St._Louis_Cardinals&oldid=879721921"& HYPERLINK "https://en.wikipedia.org/w/index.php?title= St._Louis_Cardinals&oldid=879721921"old id=879721921

Surrey. (2019). In *Wikipedia*. Retrieved from https://en.wikipedia.org/w/index.php?title=S urrey HYPERLINK "https://en.wikipedia.org/w/index.php?title= Surrey&oldid=881863065"& HYPERLINK "https://en.wikipedia.org/w/index.php?title= Surrey&oldid=881863065"oldid=88186306 5

Taiwan. (2019). In *Wikipedia*. Retrieved from https://en.wikipedia.org/w/index.php?title=T aiwan HYPERLINK "https://en.wikipedia.org/w/index.php?title=

Taiwan&oldid=880750911"& HYPERLINK "https://en.wikipedia.org/w/index.php?title= Taiwan&oldid=880750911"oldid=88075091 1

Toronto Blue Jays. (2019). In *Wikipedia*. Retrieved from https://en.wikipedia.org/w/index.php?title=T oronto_Blue_Jays HYPERLINK "https://en.wikipedia.org/w/index.php?title= Toronto_Blue_Jays&oldid=881277434"& HYPERLINK "https://en.wikipedia.org/w/index.php?title= Toronto_Blue_Jays&oldid=881277434"oldi d=881277434

United Kingdom of Great Britain and Ireland. (2019). In *Wikipedia*. Retrieved from https://en.wikipedia.org/w/index.php?title= United_Kingdom_of_Great_Britain_and_Ire land HYPERLINK "https://en.wikipedia.org/w/index.php?title= United_Kingdom_of_Great_Britain_and_Ire land&oldid=881556454"& HYPERLINK "https://en.wikipedia.org/w/index.php?title= United_Kingdom_of_Great_Britain_and_Ire land&oldid=881556454"oldid=881556454

Venezuelan Professional Baseball League. (2019). In *Wikipedia*. Retrieved from https://en.wikipedia.org/w/index.php?title= Venezuelan_Professional_Baseball_League HYPERLINK

"https://en.wikipedia.org/w/index.php?title=
Venezuelan_Professional_Baseball_League
&oldid=880679701"&   HYPERLINK
"https://en.wikipedia.org/w/index.php?title=
Venezuelan_Professional_Baseball_League
&oldid=880679701"oldid=880679701

Women's baseball. (2019). In *Wikipedia*. Retrieved from
https://en.wikipedia.org/w/index.php?title=
Women%27s_baseball   HYPERLINK
"https://en.wikipedia.org/w/index.php?title=
Women%27s_baseball&oldid=876678616"
&   HYPERLINK
"https://en.wikipedia.org/w/index.php?title=
Women%27s_baseball&oldid=876678616"o
ldid=876678616

World Baseball Classic. (2019). In *Wikipedia*. Retrieved
from
https://en.wikipedia.org/w/index.php?title=
World_Baseball_Classic   HYPERLINK
"https://en.wikipedia.org/w/index.php?title=
World_Baseball_Classic&oldid=880211084
"&   HYPERLINK
"https://en.wikipedia.org/w/index.php?title=
World_Baseball_Classic&oldid=880211084
"oldid=880211084

World Baseball Softball Confederation. (2019). In
    Wikipedia.   Retrieved   from
    https://en.wikipedia.org/w/index.php?title=
    World_Baseball_Softball_Confederation

HYPERLINK
"https://en.wikipedia.org/w/index.php?title=
World_Baseball_Softball_Confederation&ol
did=879512849"&   HYPERLINK
"https://en.wikipedia.org/w/index.php?title=
World_Baseball_Softball_Confederation&ol
did=879512849"oldid=879512849